"Then I knew we had won
something they could
never take away—
something I could leave
to our children—
and they, the

SALT OF THE EARTH,

would inherit it."

SCREENPLAY *by Michael Wilson*
COMMENTARY *by Deborah Silverton Rosenfelt*

SALT OF THE EARTH

THE FEMINIST PRESS
at The City University of New York
New York

Published by the Feminist Press at the City University of New York
The Graduate Center, 365 Fifth Avenue, Suite 5406, New York, NY 10016
feministpress.org

Library of Congress Cataloging in Publication Data

Wilson, Michael, 1914-1978
    Salt of the earth.

    Includes bibliographical references.
       1. Strikes and lockouts—Zinc mining—New Mexico—Drama. I. Salt of the earth
(motion picture) II. Rosenfelt, Deborah Silverton.
PN1997.S14   1978   812'.5'4   78-4212   ISBN 0-912670-45-2

For nontheatrical bookings of the film in the United States and Canada, contact: Macmillan Films, Inc., 34 MacQuesten Parkway South, Mount Vernon, NY 10550; phone (914) 664-5051.

For information about international distribution rights contact: JAD Films International, Inc., 405 Park Avenue, New York, NY 10022; phone (212) 751-2624.

Grateful acknowledgment to Bunny Boyd and Bob Greenberg of the audio-visual department, State University of New York at Old Westbury, for running the film for us and for lending us the department's print to make enlargements for this book.

    With special acknowledgments to
    Joan Kelly and Rose Rubin for their kind assistance.

09 08 07 06 05 04 03   8 7 6 5 4

ACKNOWLEDGMENTS

Much of the material in the commentary in this book comes from interviews and conversations with the people who created *Salt of the Earth*, who took part in the struggle that inspired it, or who inherited its story from their parents. Their graciousness made this project a pleasure from start to finish. Their experience and knowledge made it an education. They are Robert Ames, Sonja Dahl Biberman, Juan Chacón, Virginia Chacón, Virginia Derr Chambers, Paul Jarrico, Sylvia Jarrico, Clinton Jencks, Muriel Jencks, Leo Hurwitz, Joan Laird, Ben Margolis, Fina Marrufo, Reynaldo Marrufo, Benigno Móntez, Paul Perlin, Mariana Ramírez, Rosaura Revueltas, Gale Sondergaard, Anita Torres, Maurice Travis, Esperanza Chacón Villagrán, Michael Wilson, Rebecca Wilson, Zelma Wilson, and Morrie Wright.

I owe special debts to Paul Jarrico, who, in addition to spending hours of his time with me in interviews, also supplied me with the chronology which is excerpted in this book, stills from the film, an accurate version of the credits, and a portfolio of reviews and other materials; and to Esperanza Chacón Villagrán and her husband Raúl, who shared their home with me in New Mexico. Mario Barrera, Larry Ceplair, David Talbot, Harriet Tanzman, and Barbara Zheutlin were generous with materials and insights from their own research. I am deeply indebted for extensive comments and editorial suggestions on various drafts of this manuscript, as well as for encouragement and support, to Ellen Cantarow, Larry Ceplair, John McFaul, David Peck, Liz Phillips, Clancy Sigal, and again, Paul Jarrico. The mother-daughter team of Virginia Derr Chambers (formerly Virginia Jencks) and Linda Rageh provided not only informative and demanding comments on the manuscript-in-progress but also an unpublished essay on the events surrounding *Salt of the Earth*. I am also grateful for the careful reading and thoughtful responses of Emily Abel, Joan Laird, Louise Lamphere, Sara Silverton, Peg Strobel, and Jack Stuart.

I owe information and ideas to talks by and discussions with many others —activists and scholars, filmmakers and cultural critics, especially Stanley Aronowitz, Dorothy Healey, and Robert Rosen. Many of these sessions were sponsored by the Los Angeles Socialist Media Group. This work would not have been possible without the support of my friends in the women's studies program at California State University, Long Beach, or without the continuing dialogue with and help from the other members of my living collective, Claudia Fonda-Bonardi, Peter Fonda-Bonardi, Marty Hittelman, Maggie Magee, and Daniel Riesenfeld.

This project was partially supported by a Faculty Summer Fellowship and a sabbatical leave from California State University, Long Beach.

Deborah Silverton Rosenfelt

TABLE OF CONTENTS

SALT OF THE EARTH

MAKING THE FILM

SALT OF THE EARTH

To the mining families
of Grant County,
New Mexico. — *M.W.*

AND

In memory of Michael Wilson,
who died in April 1978,
shortly before
this book was published. — *D.S.R.*

SALT OF THE EARTH

Screenplay by Michael Wilson

Fade in (before titles): Ext., Quintero backyard. Medium shot, day. A woman at work chopping wood. Though her back is to Camera, we sense her weariness in toil by the set of her shoulders. A five-year-old girl is helping the woman, gathering kindling. Over this scene comes the first title. A guitar dominates the musical theme. The motif is grave, nostalgic.

Ext., Quintero backyard. A series of shots, day. As successive titles appear, each is matched by a view of the woman at her chores. Though at no time do we see her face, we begin to gather that she is large with child. The woman carries the load of wood to an outdoor fire, staggering under its weight, the little girl following with a box of kindling. . . . The woman feeds wood into the fire, on top of which is a washtub. . . . She scrubs clothes in the tub, bowed to the work, the little girl watching. . . . She wrings out articles of clothing, hanging them on a clothesline, the little girl helping gravely.

Ext., Quintero backyard. Medium close shot, day. As the last title fades, the woman continues hanging the wash and for the first time we see her face: a mask of suppression, a chiselled yet eroded beauty, the eyes hooded, smoldering. At the same time, though her lips do not move, we hear her voice: grave, nostalgic, cadenced, like the music of the guitar, inflecting the melody of Mexican-American speech.

> Glossary. *Ext:* outdoor shot; *int:* indoor shot; *o.s.:* out of scene; *f.g.:* foreground; *b.g.:* background; *pan:* panoramic, or panning, shot (camera pivots).

Woman's voice: How shall I begin my story that has no beginning?

Medium full shot. The clothes billowing in the wind as the woman hangs them up.

Woman's voice: My name is Esperanza, Esperanza Quintero. I am a miner's wife.

Ext., front of the Quintero cottage. Full shot, day. It is a small clapboard dwelling surrounded by a picket fence. Flowers are blooming outside the fence. Beyond this house similar cottages can be seen, strung out along a dirt road.

Esperanza's voice: This is our home. The house is not ours. But the flowers... the flowers are ours.

Ext., Zinc Town. Vista shot, day. We see several small stores, a gas station, scattered frame and adobe shacks, and in deep b.g. a Catholic church.

Esperanza's voice: This is my village. When I was a child, it was called San Marcos.

Fuller vista shot, including the mine on a hilltop. The mine dominates the town like a volcano. Its vast cone of waste has engulfed most of the vegetation on the hill and seems to threaten the town itself.

Esperanza's voice: The Anglos changed the name to Zinc Town. Zinc Town, New Mexico, U.S.A.

Ext., church cemetery. Medium shot, day. An ancient graveyard beside a Catholic church.

Esperanza's voice: Our roots go deep in this place, deeper than the pines, deeper than the mine shaft.

Ext., countryside. Long pan shot, day. We see great scudding clouds and the jagged skyline of a mountain spur. The mountain is scarred and pitted by old diggings. The lower slope is a skirt of waste, the grey powdery residue of an abandoned mine.

Esperanza's voice: In these arroyos my great-grandfather raised cattle before the Anglos ever came.

Close shot: a sign attached to a fence. It reads: PROPERTY OF DELAWARE ZINC. INC.

2

Vista shot: the zinc mine in the distance.

> **Esperanza's voice:** The land where the mine stands—that was owned by my husband's own grandfather.

Closer shot, featuring the mine head. At closer range we see the head frame, power house and Administration Building.

> **Esperana's voice:** Now it belongs to the company. Eighteen years my husband has given to that mine.

Int., mine. Close shot. Ramón Quintero at work. He is lighting fuses of dynamite charges which are packed into the rock face of a narrow drift. There are a dozen such fuses. The drift is lighted only by the lamp on Ramón's hat.

> **Esperanza's voice:** Living half his life with dynamite and darkness.

Close-up: a fuse. It sputters, runs.

The drift, wider angle to include Ramón's wild face as he turns and runs. We see only a bobbing lamp and the long shadow of a man running. We see a flash of light, hear muffled thunder.

Ext., Quintero backyard. Medium shot, day. Esperanza has paused a moment in her work, looking off toward the mine with a worried frown. Now she picks up the heavy clothes-basket and walks toward the cottage. The little Estella is not in sight.

> **Esperanza's voice:** Who can say where it began, my story? I do not know. But this day I remember as the beginning of an end.

Int., Quintero kitchen. Medium shot, day. It is no more than a narrow passageway, dominated by an ancient wood-burning stove. There is no running water. Esperanza sets the basket down beside an ironing board, picks up an iron from the stove and tests it with a moistened finger.

> **Esperanza's voice:** It was my Saint's Day. I was thirty-five years old. A day of celebration. And I was seven months gone with my third child.

Estella has run into shot, presenting her mother with a rose. Esperanza pins the rose in Estella's hair, with a small smile, then returns to her ironing. As she irons, her face becomes more and more desolate.

Esperanza's voice: And on that day—I remember I had a wish...a thought so sinful...

In a convulsive gesture her fingers go to her lips. She drops the iron and hurries from the kitchen.

Int., parlor. Medium close shot at shrine. We see only a corner of the small cramped parlor where Esperanza, with bowed head and clenched hands, stands before a shrine to the Virgin.

Esperanza's voice: ...a thought so evil that I prayed God to forgive me for it. I wished...I wished that my child would never be born. No. Not into this world.

Esperanza covers her face with her hands. The little girl enters scene, stares gravely at her.

Estella: Are you sick, Mama?
Esperanza: No, Estellita.
Estella: Are you sad? *(As Esperanza doesn't answer.)* Are we going to church? For your confession?
Esperanza: Later. When I finish the ironing. *(She goes out.)*

Full shot: kitchen. As Esperanza starts ironing again, her son Luís enters by the back door. A handsome boy of thirteen, but now panting and bedraggled, he pours himself a glass of water and gulps it down. Esperanza watches him sidelong.

Esperanza: Fighting again? *(No response.)* With those Anglo kids?
Luís: Aah, they think they're tough.
Esperanza: But you promised you wouldn't.
Luís *(unrepentant):* Papa says if an Anglo makes fun of you to let him have it.

Esperanza suddenly seizes his shoulder, spinning him around as if about to slap him, crying simultaneously:

Esperanza: Never mind what your papa...

For the first time she (and we) see that the boy's mouth is bleeding. Her anger is washed away in a wave of concern, and she picks up a cloth and wipes the blood.

Esperanza: Hold still...does it hurt?

Luís *(pulling away):* Naah.

He spies a birthday cake on the drainboard, sticks his finger in the icing.

Luís: How come the cake?

Esperanza grabs the cake, puts it in the cupboard.

Esperanza: Never mind. Go get your father when he comes off shift. Tell him to come straight home.

Glad to be released, the boy darts off as we:

Dissolve to: ext., Delaware Zinc Co. mine. Long shot, day. In deep b.g. stands the head frame of the mine. We hear one shrill blast of a steam whistle, and as this sound dies away we hear the rattling hoist and conveyor belt, punctuated occasionally by the loud crash of ore from the bucket into the crusher. In right f.g. stands the Administration Building, a long wooden bungalow.

Moving with a group of miners, striding in a body toward the Administration Building. They appear angry and determined. Ramón Quintero is in the lead. The others are Antonio Morales, Alfredo Díaz, Sebastian Prieto, Jenkins and Kalinsky. They all wear tin hats and grimy work clothes.

Another angle, featuring Administration Building, as Chief Foreman Barton emerges from the Superintendent's office. He wears khaki and a Stetson. Seeing the approaching miners, he moves out to intercept them.

Group shot: Barton and miners. The miners stop as Barton, hands in his hip pockets, blocks their way. Barton is a rangy Texan with a perpetual half-smile on his lips. Ramón, the miners' spokesman, is rugged, handsome, younger in appearance than Esperanza, although he is a year older. There is a smoldering intensity in his manner and speech. During the following the boy Luís enters scene, coming up behind his father. The men ignore him.

Barton: Hear you had a little trouble, Quintero. Defective fuse? *(Ramón nods.)* Well, you're all in one piece. So what's the beef?
Ramón: You know the beef. This new rule of yours, that we work alone. We're taking it up with the Super.

Barton: Super's busy—with your Negotiatin' Committee.
Ramón: So much the better.

He starts off, but Barton blocks his path again.

Another angle.

Barton: Now wait a minute. Super's the one made the rule. *He* ain't gonna give you no helper.
Ramón: He will if he wants us to go on blasting.

The other miners step forward in support of Ramón. They protest excitedly, their speeches overlapping.

Antonio: Listen, Mr. Barton—there's blood in that mine. The blood of my friends. All because they had to work alone...
Jenkins: That's how ya get splattered over the rocks, when there's nobody to help you check your fuses...
Alfredo *(breaking in):*... And nobody to warn the other men to stay clear.
Barton: Warning's the shift foreman's job.

Ramón: Foreman wants to get the ore out. Miner wants to get his brothers out. In one piece.

Barton: You work alone, savvy? You can't handle the job, I'll find someone who can.

Ramón: Who? A scab?

Barton: An American.

He exits. Ramón stands there, taut.

Dissolve to: Int., kitchen of Quintero cottage. Full shot, evening. Esperanza enters from the parlor with some dirty dishes followed by Estella, who carries her own plate. As Esperanza picks up the coffee pot, she spies Estella holding a candle over the frosting of the cake on the drainboard.

Estella: Mama, can I put the candles...

Esperanza *(a fierce whisper):* Hush... not a word about the cake, hear?

Int., parlor. Full shot. The room is small, cramped. The plaster walls are cracked and peeling. Most of the furnishings are faded and old. Nevertheless, the cottage is tidy and gives evidence of considerable care. A dilapidated couch is covered with a fine Mexican blanket. In one corner of the room stands a shrine to the Virgin. A vase of fresh-cut flowers stands on the mantelpiece beneath a framed portrait of Benito Juárez. The only item of splendor in the room is a high-polished radio-phonograph console. Over scene we hear a tin-pan-alley compost of "Western" music sung by cowboy entertainers.

Ramón sits with Luís at a small table near the kitchen door. Esperanza enters with the coffee pot, pours his coffee. Estella follows her, climbing onto her father's lap.

> **Luís:** Papa... is there gonna be a strike?

Ramón ignores the question, brooding. Esperanza, who would also like to hear an answer, watches his face as he sips his coffee.

> **Esperanza** *(finally, timidly)*: Ramón...I don't like to bother you ...but the store lady said if we don't make a payment on the radio this month, they'll take it away.

Ramón's forehead falls against his upraised palm, as if to say it's too much to bear. The little girl looks at him gravely.

> **Esperanza:** We're only one payment behind. I argued with her. It isn't right.
>
> **Ramón** *(softly, imploring heaven)*: It isn't right, she says. Was it right that we bought this... this instrument?

He rises, holding Estella.

> **Ramón:** But you had to have it, didn't you? It was so nice to listen to.
>
> **Esperanza** *(quietly)*: I listen to it. Every night. When you're out to the beer parlor.

Ignoring this mild rebuke, Ramón crosses to the radio. Camera pans with him. He glares at the console, mimicking an announcer's commercial.

> **Ramón:** "No money down. Easy term payments." I tell you something: this installment plan, it's the curse of the working man.

He slams his coffee cup down on the console, sets his daughter down and goes to the kitchen. Esperanza quickly polishes the console where he struck it.

8

Int., kitchen. Medium close shot. Ramón strips to the waist, pours some water from the tub on the stove into a pan on the drainboard. Esperanza appears in the doorway, watching him, her heart sinking. Her fingers go to her lips in a characteristic gesture.

> **Esperanza:** Where you going?
> **Ramón:** Got to talk to the brothers.

Esperanza bites her finger, trying to hide her disappointment. Ramón bends over the pan to wash. He has not noticed the cake. Esperanza picks it up quickly, hides it in a cupboard. Ramón splashes his face and neck with water, looks up in irritation.

> **Ramón:** This water's cold again.
> **Esperanza:** I'm sorry. The fire's gone out.

She begins to stoke the stove.

> **Ramón:** Forget it.
> **Esperanza:** Forget it? I chop wood for the stove five times a day. Every time I remember. I remember that across the tracks the Anglo miners have hot water. In pipes. And bathrooms. Inside.
> **Ramón** *(bitterly)*: Do you think I like living this way? What do you want of me?!

He reaches for a towel. Esperanza hands him one.

> **Esperanza:** But if your union . . . if you're asking for better conditions . . . why can't you ask for decent plumbing, too?

Frustrated, evasive, Ramón turns away, buttoning his shirt.

> **Ramón:** We did. It got lost in the shuffle.
> **Esperanza:** What?
> **Ramón:** *(shrugging)*: We can't get everything at once. Right now we've got more important demands.
> **Esperanza** *(timidly)*: What's more important than sanitation?
> **Ramón** *(flaring)*: The safety of the men—that's more important! Five accidents this week—all because of speed-up. You're a woman, you don't know what it's like up there.

She bows her head without answering and picks up the heavy tub of water on the stove. Unassisted, she lugs it to the dishpan in the sink and fills it. Ramón begins to comb his hair, adding in a more subdued tone:

Ramón: First we got to get equality on the job. Then we'll work on these other things. Leave it to the men.

Esperanza: *(quietly):* I see. The men. You'll strike, maybe, for your demands—but what the wives want, that comes later, always later.

Ramón *(darkly):* Now don't start talking about the union again.

Esperanza *(a shrug of defeat):* What has it got me, your union?

Ramón looks at her in amazement, not with anger, but with deep concern.

Ramón: Esperanza, have you forgotten what it was like . . . before the union came? *(Points toward parlor.)* When Estella was a baby, and we couldn't even afford a doctor when she got sick? It was for our families! We met in graveyards to build that union!

Esperanza *(lapsing into despair):* All right. Have your strike. I'll have my baby. But no hospital will take me, because I'll be a striker's wife. The store will cut off our credit, and the kids will go hungry. And we'll get behind on the payments again, and then they'll come and take away the radio . . .

Ramón *(furiously):* Is that all you care about? That radio? Can't you think of anything except yourself?

Esperanza *(breaking):* If I think of myself it's because you never think of me. Never. Never. Never . . .

Reverse angle, shooting toward parlor. She covers her face with her hands, begins to sob violently. Ramón seizes her arms, shakes her. In b.g. we see the two children still at table.

Ramón: Stop it! The children are watching. Stop it!

Esperanza *(sobbing uncontrollably):* Never . . . never . . . never!

Ramón: Aaah, what's the use?

He drops her arms abruptly, almost flinging her aside, and stalks out of the kitchen, out of the house. Esperanza remains leaning against the cupboard, sobbing. Camera holds. The boy Luís rises from the table, comes to the kitchen door, looks at his mother. Then he, too, turns and leaves the house.

Quick dissolve to: ext., beer parlor, Zinc Town. Full shot, night. The place is lighted by a neon sign. From within we hear a juke box playing ersatz Mexican music. The boy approaches the door, pauses and enters.

Int., beer parlor. Full shot, night. It is nondescript, small, dingy, dimly lighted, indistinguishable from a hundred other small-town bars. A half-dozen miners, including Antonio Morales, Sebastian Prieto, and Alfredo Díaz, stand at the bar rail drinking beer. The bartender is an Anglo. We hear:

> We know it's not safe for miners to work alone! The boss will always tell you things like that!

Luís has reached a post near a table at the far end of the room. Four men are seated around the table: Sal Ruíz, Frank Barnes, Charley Vidal and Ramón—whose back is to Camera. Sal is drinking coffee; the other three are drinking beer. Luís stops, and as Camera moves in on group we pick up:

> **Ramón** *(angrily):* They don't work alone in other mines! Anglos *always* work in pairs. So why should I risk my life? Because I'm only a Mexican?
> **Sal and Charley:** But that's in the demands . . . we're negotiating . . .
> **Ramón:** Three months of negotiations! And nothing happens! *(Indicates Frank.)* Even with Brother Barnes here from the International, what've we got? *(Ticks them off.)* No raise. No seniority. No safety code. Nothing.

Reverse angle, shooting toward Ramón. The boy Luís can be seen in b.g., but everyone ignores him. During the previous speech Sebastian Prieto and Antonio Morales have approached the table. Antonio sets a fresh bottle of beer before Ramón.

> **Antonio:** Take a drink. Calm down!
> **Ramón** *(to Frank, ignoring Antonio):* I say we gotta take action. Now.
> **Frank:** Rest of the men feel like you?

Ramón glances over his shoulder at the standing miners. Sebastian glances uncertainly at Antonio.

> **Antonio** *(firmly):* He speaks for all of us.
> **Charley:** Ever stop to think maybe they want us to strike?
> **Ramón:** Don't horse *me*. Price of zinc's never been higher. They don't want no strike—not with their war boom on.
> **Frank:** Then why's the company hanging tough? They've signed contracts with other locals—why not this one?
> **Ramón** *(striking the table):* Because most of us here are Mexican-

Americans! Because we want equality with Anglo miners—the same pay, the same conditions.

Frank: Exactly. And equality's the one thing the bosses can't afford. The biggest club they have over the Anglo locals is, "Well—at least you get more than the Mexicans."

Ramón: Okay, so discrimination hurts the Anglo too, *but it hurts me more.* And I've had enough of it!

Sal: But you don't pull a strike when the bosses want it—so they can smash your union. You wait till you're ready, so you can win.

Ramón: Do the bosses wait? No sanitation. So my kids get sick. Does the company doctor wait? Twenty bucks. So we miss one payment on the radio I bought for my wife. Does the company store wait? "Pay—or we take it away." Why they in such a hurry, the bosses' store? They're trying to scare us, that's why—to make us afraid to move. To hang on to what we got—and like it! Well, I don't like it...I'm not scared...and I'm fed up—to here! *(His hand goes a foot over his head.)*

Antonio: Hey, Ramón—¡te buscan!

With a jerk of his head he indicates Luís. Ramón turns around, spots his son. He rises, frowning, and moves toward him.

Two shot: Ramón and Luís.

> **Ramón** *(roughly):* What are you doing here? *(Suddenly worried.)* Something wrong with Mama?
> **Luís** *(deadpan):* I thought maybe you forgot.
> **Ramón:** Forgot what?
> **Luís:** It's Mama's Saint's Day.

Ramón is stunned, as though from a slap across the face. At last he works up a travesty of a grin.

> **Ramón:** You think I forgot? I was planning a surprise...

Ramón turns back to the men. Camera follows him, holding on the group.

> **Ramón** *(chuckling):* What a kid. He can't wait. It's my wife's Saint's Day. I was gonna ask you, brothers—how about a mañanita, huh?

> **Ad libs** (eagerly):
> Sure.
> What time?
> The later the better...
> Wait'll she's asleep...

Dissolve to: Ext., Quintero cottage. Full shot, night. No lights are visible in the cottage, or in those adjoining it. A cluster of men, women and children can be seen in the front yard, serenading by moonlight. The song is called "Las Mañanitas." Two of the men are strumming guitars.

Closer angle: the serenaders. They include Ramón and Luís, Antonio and Luz Morales, Sal and Consuelo Ruíz, Charley and Teresa Vidal, Frank and Ruth Barnes, Alfredo Díaz and his wife, Sebastian Prieto and a silver-haired old lady of great dignity, Mrs. Salazar. The children range from two to fifteen, and there are many of them. Except for the youngest they sing as lustily as their parents.

Int., bedroom, Quintero house. Full shot, night. The small bedroom is partitioned by a screen, separating the children's cots from the parents' bed. A crucifix hangs over the bed. The room is feebly lighted by one small lamp. Esperanza lies in bed, an arm flung across her eyes. The sound of the singing comes faintly over scene. Camera moves in slowly on Esperanza. Her arm falls to her side. She opens her eyes. She listens, motionless.

Another angle: the bedroom, as Estella emerges from behind the screen and climbs onto her mother's bed, with a kind of sleepy-eyed wonder.

> **Estella:** Why are they singing, Mama?
> **Esperanza:** They are singing for me.
> **Estella:** Can we light the candles now? On the cake?
> **Esperanza** (smiles): Yes. We will light the candles.

Suddenly she flings back the bed covers, reaches for a dressing gown and puts it on.

Ext., Quintero cottage. Full shot, night. The lights come up in the parlor. The front door opens, revealing Esperanza and Estella. They smile, remain in the open doorway as the serenaders go into a final chorus. The song ends in laughter and applause. They swarm into the house.

13

Int., parlor. Full shot, night. A merry bedlam, with Esperanza receiving her guests. Sal Ruíz starts up a bawdy folk song on his guitar. He is urged on by Charley Vidal's wild falsetto. Antonio lugs a case of beer into the house and immediately starts uncapping it, passing foaming bottles to everyone. The women gather around Esperanza, embracing her, wishing her a happy birthday in English and Spanish. Ramón is the last to enter.

Closer angle, featuring Esperanza and Ramón confronting each other in the center of the room. Ramón gazes at her in silence, repentant. She returns his gaze, for the moment oblivious of her guests, who gracefully withdraw from the situation. Esperanza's eyes fill with tears, she smiles tremulously, and her fingers go to her lips.

    Esperanza: I . . . I must get dressed.

She flees from the room. Ramón follows her, gesturing to men to keep on with their singing.

Int., bedroom. Two shot: Ramón and Esperanza. He puts his arms around her, tentatively. Her forehead falls against his shoulder.

    Esperanza: I did not mean to weep again. Why should I weep for joy?
    Ramón: I'm a fool.
    Esperanza: No, no . . .

She raises her head, brushing her cheek against his.

    Esperanza: Was it expensive, the beer?
    Ramón: Antonio paid for it.
    Esperanza: Forgive me . . . for saying you never thought of me.
    Ramón (with effort): I did forget. Luís told me.

Grateful for his honesty, she pulls his head down, kisses him. He returns her kiss passionately.

Dissolve to: a montage, showing Esperanza chopping wood outside her kitchen door. The carefree guitar music of the mañanita carries over scene—and Esperanza pauses in her labors, seeming to hear it again.

    Esperanza's voice: All the next week I kept thinking about my ma-ñanita. I had never had so nice a party . . .

The image on the screen gives way to another as Esperanza recollects the occasion: we see Esperanza and Estella blowing out the candles on the birthday cake, surrounded by their beaming guests.

    Esperanza's voice: It was like a song running through my mind, a humming in my heart, a daydream to lighten the long days' work . . .

Ext., Quintero backyard. Close shot: Esperanza bending over a large tub, scrubbing clothes. She pauses, smiles reflectively.

    Esperanza's voice: We forgot our troubles at the mañanita—even Ramón . . .

A new image is superimposed on the screen. Now we see Ramón dancing with Consuelo Ruíz, while Esperanza looks on, smiling.

> **Esperanza's voice:** I couldn't dance that night—not in my condition. But I wasn't really jealous when he danced with the others . . . because it was good just to see him smile again . . .

Ext., Quintero yard, clothesline. Full shot, day. Esperanza and Luz are hanging clothes and talking across the fence between them. Their two children are playing together in f.g.

> **Esperanza's voice:** And then one morning I was hanging out my wash.

Another angle: the yard, shooting toward front gate. In deep b.g. we see three women enter the Morales yard and approach Luz. They beckon to Esperanza.

> **Esperanza's voice:** And while we were talking the ladies came. They were a kind of delegation. It was about the sanitation, they said . . .

Closer angle: the group at fence, as Esperanza comes over. Throughout this scene the two children climb up, down and sidways on the fence in an intricate little geometric dance. Luz goes on hanging up her clothes. We see the delegation talking earnestly to Esperanza and Luz but we hear only:

> **Esperanza's voice:** The Anglo miners have bathrooms and hot running water, Consuelo said, why shouldn't we?
> **Esperanza** (sighing): I know, I spoke to Ramón about it—only a week ago.
> **Ruth:** And what did he say?
> **Esperanza:** They dropped it from their demands.
> **Consuelo** (sighs): Es lo de siempre.
> **Teresa** (the militant): We got to make them understand—make the men face up to it. (To Ruth) Show her the sign.

Another angle: the group, as Ruth lifts up a placard, hitherto unseen, which she has been holding at her side. It reads: WE WANT SANITATION—NOT DISCRIMINATION.

> **Consuelo:** We'll make a lot of signs like this. Then we'll get all the wives together and go right up to the mine.

Esperanza: To the mine?

Teresa: Sure. Where they're negotiating. In the company office. We'll go up there and picket the place.

Consuelo: Then both sides will see we mean business.

Esperanza *(thunderstruck)*: A picket line? Of . . . of ladies?

Ruth: Sure. Why not?

Luz flings a pair of damp pants on the clothesline without hanging them up.

Luz: You can count me in.

Esperanza *(scandalized)*: Luz!

Luz: Listen, we ought to be in the woodchoppers' union. Chop wood for breakfast. Chop wood to wash his clothes. Chop wood, heat the iron. Chop wood, scrub the floor. Chop wood, cook his dinner. And you know what he'll say when he gets home. *(Mimics Antonio.)* "What you been doing all day? Reading the funny papers?"

The women laugh softly, all except Esperanza.

Teresa: Come on, Esperanza—how about it? We got to.

Esperanza: No. No. I can't. If Ramón ever found me on a picket line . . . *(Her voice trails off.)*

Consuelo: He'd what? Beat you?

Esperanza: No . . . No . . .

Suddenly we hear, from far off, five short blasts of a steam whistle. The women fall silent instantly, listening. Then it comes again. Five short blasts.

Ext., mine head. Long shot, day. We can see little puffs of steam from the whistle on the head frame, and again we hear five short blasts.

Back to the women, frozen, apprehensive. Luz expels the word that has already crossed their minds.

Luz: . . . accidente . . .

She grabs her son from off the fence and hurries with him to the gate and out on the road. The others begin to follow, as though magnetized. The signal continues over:

A series of shots, showing women emerging from their houses, looking off at the mine. Women strung out along the dirt road leading to the

17

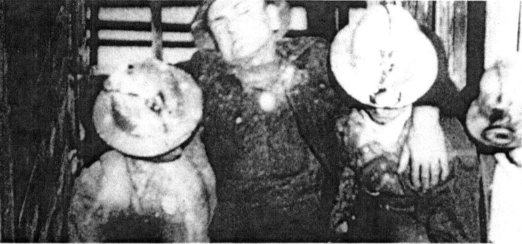

mine. Esperanza, slowed down by her unborn child, tagging along behind, holding Estella's hand.

Ext., mine head. Medium long shot, day. Men are scurrying toward the head frame from all directions. Two of them carry a stretcher. At this distance the whistle blast is much louder.

Ext., Administration Office. Medium long shot, day. The union negotiators, Ruíz, Vidal and Barnes, emerge from the company office and walk swiftly toward the mine head. Superintendent Alexander and two company men follow.

Ext., road leading toward mine. Long panning shot. An ancient, dusty ambulance, its siren wailing, bounces along the narrow road leading to the mine. The advancing women make way for it.

Ext., head frame of mine. Medium shot, at hoist. A cluster of miners wait tensely around the hoist as the cage rises to ground level. Several miners wearing tin hats are crowded inside the cage, but their faces are so grimy we cannot make out who they are.

Medium long shot: women and children who have stopped on a little knoll at some distance from the mine head. They are looking down at:

The mine head, from their angle. So many men gather around the injured man or men that we can still not distinguish them. But we see a body placed on a stretcher. Two men carry it toward the waiting ambulance.

Back to women. Close group shot. One woman breaks away and plunges down the hill. The others heave a collective sigh—a sigh of relief, anguish, compassion.

Luz: It's Mr. Kalinsky.

Rear of ambulance. Medium shot. A large number of miners are milling about. The injured man is lifted into the ambulance and the doors are shut. Just then Mrs. Kalinsky runs up. She pounds on the doors.

Mrs. Kalinsky (*hysterically*): Let me see him! Let me see him!

Several miners try to calm her. They lead her away as the ambulance starts up.

Ad libs:
Now Mrs. Kalinsky, he's gonna be all right...
His leg's broken, that's all...
Come on now, you can see him in the hospital...

The milling crowd. Another angle, as Superintendent Alexander comes up to the chief foreman. Ramón is close by. He is dirty, sweating, furious.

Alexander: How did it happen?
Barton: He wandered into a drift—when this fellow was blasting. *(He indicates Ramón.)*
Ramón *(seething):* I told you it would happen. It's bound to happen when a man works alone!
Alexander *(to Ramón):* Why didn't you give a warning signal?

Ramón *(indicates Barton, bitterly):* Your foreman says that's a foreman's job.
Barton: I checked the drift just before he blasted. It was all clear. The man must have been asleep or something.
Ramón: You weren't even there. You were back at the station. Kalinsky told me—
Barton *(softly):* You're a liar, Pancho. A no-good, dirty...

Ramón lunges at him. Barton fends him off. Ramón keeps boring in, but Sal Ruíz and Frank Barnes grab him. We hear an angry bedlam.

Ad libs *(in Spanish and English):*
¡Déjame! I'll kill him!
Hold him! Hold him!...
¡Basta, Ramón!
All right, all right. Break it up...
Alexander *(pointing at Ramón):* You, there. Get a hold on yourself. A man's been hurt. I'm as sorry about it as you are. Savvy?

Ramón finally quiets down. By now the miners have formed a ragged phalanx in b.g. The three union negotiators, Ramón, the Superintendent and the Chief Foreman form a group in f.g. Alexander speaks to all of them.

Alexander: Accidents are costly to everyone—and to the company most of all. *(Glances at his watch.)* And now, I see no reason to treat the occasion like a paid holiday. Suppose we all get back to work.

He takes a couple of steps, stops, noting that no one has moved.

> **Alexander** (*an order*): Mr. Barton.
> **Barton** (*a bluff approach*): All right, fellows, the excitement's over. Let's get to it.

Barton starts toward the mine head. But the men do not move. Faintly we hear mutterings in Spanish from the miners' ranks.

> **Ad libs:**
> ...'hora.
> ...Sí, yo creo que sí.

Another angle, featuring Alexander.

> **Alexander** (*exasperated, to Vidal*): What are they saying?
> **Charley:** No savvy.
> **Alexander** (*turning to Frank*): Well, Barnes? How about it? Tell them to get back to work.
> **Frank** (*grinning*): They don't work for me. I work for them.
> **Alexander** (*sharply*): Ruíz?

Wider angle, shooting toward miners. Sal Ruíz takes his time. He lights a cigarette. Then he calls out in Spanish:

> **Sal:** It's up to you, brothers.

A murmur runs through the ranks, "*sí, sí.*" Several miners glance at Ramón. Suddenly Ramón wheels, strides toward the power house, which is adjacent to the head frame of the mine. Passing through the miners' ranks, he bellows at the top of his lungs:

> **Ramón:** Cente!

Ext., power house. Close shot, at door. As the man named Cente (Vicente) sticks his head out the doorway of a galvanized tin shack, we hear a yell from off scene.

> **Ramón's voice:** ¡Apágalo!

Cente's head disappears.

22

A control board. Close shot containing several big industrial circuit breakers. Cente's hand comes up, pulls the switch.

Ext., head frame, featuring crusher. The gigantic, primary crusher, with rock rattling around in it, suddenly stops.

Ext., head frame: at conveyor, carrying small lumps of ore from the crusher. The belt stops.

Back to men. Full shot. The stillness is vast and sudden. Ramón walks back to the massed ranks of his fellow miners. He halts beside Antonio at the end of the file. No one else moves or speaks.

Closer angle: the miners' ranks. Antonio nudges Ramón, indicating something o.s. Ramón's head turns, looking off scene. One by one the heads of the other miners turn, glancing o.s.

Medium shot: foreman and superintendent standing before the silent miners. Barton realizes that the men are not looking at him, but at something above and beyond him. Barton looks over his shoulder. Alexander slowly follows suit.

From their angle, long shot: the women and children standing on the knoll above the mine. They are silent and grave. The women's skirts billow in the wind, like unfurled flags, like the tattered banners of a guerrilla band that has come to offer its services to the regular army. Fade out.

Fade in: close up: a license plate. It is a New Mexico plate, and though it is night we can make out clearly the words on the white background on the plate: LAND OF ENCHANTMENT.

Camera pulls back slowly to disclose a cowboy boot perched on a car bumper.

Camera pulls back further, disclosing a khaki-clad leg, a pearl-handled revolver in a holster—then the full figure of a deputy leaning on the fender of his car. He is picking his teeth with a matchstick and gazing at:

Ext., union hall, shooting past sheriff's car, night. The car is parked provocatively near the entrance to the building. A sign over the doorway, lighted by reflectors, identifies the place as the union hall. From within we hear the muted tumult of a packed house. In near f.g. is another parked car containing several women and children.

Esperanza's voice: That night the men held a union meeting... just to make the walk-out official.

Suddenly we hear a roar of applause from inside the hall. The door opens; Luís and a tow-headed youngster come bounding out, run toward the car, Camera panning with them.

Esperanza's voice: It didn't take them long. They voted to strike— ninety-three to five.

We see the car door open: Ruth Barnes and Teresa emerge from the front seat; Consuelo, holding a sleeping infant, gets out of the back. Esperanza is the last to appear. Estella is asleep in her arms.

Esperanza's voice: ...And Teresa said now was the time for us to go in. I didn't want to...I had never been to a union meeting. But the others said, one go, all go...

We see the women coaxng Esperanza. She follows them reluctantly toward the union hall.

Full shot, night: int., union hall as seen from the entrance. A hundred miners are packed densely on the center block of benches, facing the union officers in b.g. Sal Ruíz is presiding; Frank Barnes sits at the table beside him. Charley Vidal stands near the chairman, delivering an impassioned speech.

Charley Vidal: We have many complaints, brothers, and many demands. But they all add up to one word: Equality!

Over sound track we hear the Spanish of Charley's speech, but it is modulated to:

Esperanza's voice: The meeting was nearly over when we came in. Charley Vidal was making a speech. He said there was only one issue in this strike—equality. But the mine owners would stop at nothing to keep them from getting equality.

The hall. Another angle, including the women. The men are so intent on Charley Vidal's speech that they do not notice the entrance of the women, who tiptoe unobtrusively to the side of the room where they take seats on the unoccupied wall bench. Estella wakes up, blinking in the bright lights.

24

The hall. Full shot, featuring Charley.

> **Esperanza's voice:** He said the bosses would try to split the Anglo and Mexican-American workers and offer rewards to one man if he would sell out his brother....There was only one answer to that, Charley said—solidarity. The solidarity of working men.

Charley concludes his speech:

> **Charley Vidal:** To all this, brothers, there is only one answer, the solidarity of working men!

He sits down to loud applause which comes up over sound track. Sal Ruíz rises, bangs his gavel.

Group shot: the women. Ruth and Teresa nudge Consuelo, trying to get her to rise—but Consuelo, frightened, clings to her sleeping infant. Ruth grabs the baby and Teresa practically pushes Consuelo to her feet.

Wider angle, shooting past Sal, including women. Charley Vidal plucks at Sal's sleeve, points in the direction of the women.

> **Sal:** Yes? You ladies have an announcement?
> **Consuelo** *(haltingly)*: Well—it's not an announcement, I guess. The ladies wanted me to...
> **Voice from the floor:** Louder!
> **Sal:** Consuelo, will you speak from over here?

Painfully self-conscious, Consuelo moves toward Camera in f.g. She faces the men and begins again, nervous, but trying to speak louder.

> **Consuelo:** The ladies have been talking about sanitation...and we were thinking...if the issue is equality, like you say it is, then maybe we ought to have equality in plumbing too....

Close group shot: miners. Some appear resentful of the women's intrusion; others seem amused. Antonio whispers something to Alfredo. Alfredo laughs. Frowning, Ramón looks around at Esperanza, as he might look at a woman who entered church uncovered.

> **Consuelo's voice:** I mean, maybe it could be a strike demand... and some of the ladies thought—it might be a good idea to have a ladies' auxiliary! Well, we would like to help out...if we can....

Full shot: the hall, featuring Consuelo. Consuelo hurries back to her seat. Camera holds. We hear mild, scattered applause, and then a male falsetto giggle sets off a wave of laughter. Ruíz rises, grins sheepishly.

> **Sal:** I'm sure I can speak for all of the brothers. We appreciate the ladies offering to help, but it's getting late and I suggest we table it. The chair will entertain a motion to adjourn.
> **First miner** *(from the floor):* Move to adjourn!
> **Second miner:** Second!
> **Sal:** So ordered.

He brings down his gavel, and the meeting ends. Some of the miners break for the door, others begin to mill about. Ruth and Consuelo walk to the front of the hall. Now, in quick succession we see four vignettes.

Two shot: Sal and Consuelo. He meets her near the speaker's table, flings out his arms in a helpless gesture.

> **Sal:** Why didn't you check with me? It's embarrassing!

Two shot: Ruth and Frank. She leans across the speaker's table before Frank can rise and remarks acidly:

> **Ruth:** Why didn't you support her? You're the worst of the lot.
> **Frank:** But honey...
> **Ruth:** Or why don't you just put a sign outside? "No dogs or women allowed!"

Another part of the hall. Charley and Teresa.

> **Charley:** But Teresa, you can't push these things too fast.
> **Teresa** *(fiercely):* You were pushing all right—pushing us right back in our place.

Esperanza and Ramón, near doorway. Esperanza is holding Estella, who is asleep again. Ramón is at the rear of a group of miners filing out of the hall. As two of the miners pass Camera, we hear one say to the other:

> **First miner:** That's a pretty good idea—making sanitation one of the demands again.

As Ramón moves into f.g., he indicates with the slightest of gestures for Esperanza to follow. She obeys.

Ext., union hall. Medium panning shot, night. Ramón emerges from the hall, moves to a corner of the building in f.g. Esperanza joins him there in the darkness. Ramón speaks softly.

> **Ramón:** At least you didn't make a fool of yourself—like Consuelo.

Slow dissolve to: ext., picket line. Long establishing shot. This panorama should be as inclusive as the location site permits. Thirty or more miners march counterclockwise on a dirt road. Beyond this elliptical picket line on either side of the road are two signs: DELAWARE ZINC CO., INC.—KEEP OUT— MINERS ON STRIKE—WE WANT EQUALITY.

Though the area is unfenced, these signs mark an imaginary boundary. But access to the mine is difficult except by way of the road. To the right of the road is a steep wooded hillside. The road skirts this hill till it reaches the mountain of waste in deep b.g., then winds uphill to the knoll on which the mine stands. To the left of the road is a railroad spur and a gully. The gully is bridged by trestles, beyond which a fork of the road leads to Zinc Town. Two sheriff's cars are parked on the road near the picket post. No women are visible in this scene.

> **Esperanza's voice:** And so it began—much like any other strike. There would be no settlement, the company said, till the men returned to their jobs. But their back-to-work movement didn't work.

Wipe to: the picket line. Closer angle. Two open touring cars loaded with strike-breakers slowly approach the picket line. The lead car stops before this human wall. The pickets make no menacing gestures, but they are ominous in massed silence.

> **Esperanza's voice:** And so the company recruited a few strike-breakers from out of town.

We see the lead car make a U-turn and withdraw the way it came. It is followed by the second car.

> **Esperanza's voice:** But they usually lost their nerve when they saw the size of the picket line.

Another angle. Featuring Sheriff's cars parked near the picket line. A half-dozen deputies stand around idly. They are khaki-clad, booted, wearing their Stetsons with the brims rolled up. They display their side-arms ostentatiously, their holsters hanging low in the fashion of storybook gunmen.

> **Esperanza's voice:** The Sheriff's men were always there. They stood around, showing off their weapons. But the men only marched, day after day, week after week. . . .

Wipe to: ext., road, outside Quintero cottage. Full shot, day. Charley Vidal and another miner stand in the back of a pick-up, distributing rations to Esperanza and Luz Morales. The small sacks contain beans, corn meal, coffee, etc.

> **Esperanza's voice:** At first it was a kind of unwritten rule that the women stay at home. The union gave us rations and we had to figure out how to feed our families on them . . .

Ext., picket line. Medium shot, day. There are fewer pickets now, and the miners, weary of the monotony, march in a more leisurely fashion. We see Mrs. Salazar (the old lady introduced at the mañanita) standing close by the picket line. She is crocheting. Ramón, the picket captain, and other miners glance uncomfortably at her.

> **Esperanza's voice:** But then one morning Mrs. Salazar went to the picket line. Her husband had been killed in a strike many years before . . . and she wanted to be there.

Wipe to: the picket line. Matching shot, on another day. Mrs. Salazar is now marching with the men. She is still crocheting. Her expression of calm determination is unchanging.

> **Esperanza's voice:** Nobody remembers just how it happened, but one day Mrs. Salazar started marching with them . . . and she kept on marching with them.

Wipe to: the picket post. Another angle. We see Teresa Vidal standng beside an old jalopy, pouring a cup of coffee for her husband.

> **Esperanza's voice:** After a while some of the women began to bring coffee for their husbands . . . and maybe a couple of tacos — because a man gets tired and hungry on picket duty . . .

Wipe to: the pickets. Group shot. Several pickets gape ravenously at Antonio as he bites into the tacos given him by Luz.

Esperanza's voice: It was about that time the union decided maybe they'd better set up a Ladies Auxiliary after all.

Wipe to: the picket post. Another angle and another day. A number of miners have turned carpenter, erecting a shack of scrap lumber and galvanized tin close by the picket line. Several women have set up a table outside the unfinished shack on which we see a pot of beans, a coffee pot, etc. Esperanza is not among them.

Wipe to: ext., coffee shack. Medium shot, day. The shack is now complete. We see Ramón approach the doorway, where a woman hands him a cup of coffee. He tastes it, makes a wry face.

Esperanza's voice: I didn't come to the lines at first. My time was near—and besides, Ramón didn't approve. But Ramón is a man who loves good coffee. And he swore the other ladies made it taste like zinc sludge . . .

Wipe to matching shot: the coffee shack, featuring Esperanza. Standing in the doorway, her pregnancy is more evident than ever. But her face is alight with one of her rare smiles as she pours a cup of coffee and hands it to Ramón. Estella can be seen peeking out from behind her mother's skirt.

Esperanza's voice: So one day I made the coffee...

Camera pans with Ramón as he strolls back toward the picket line, sipping his coffee.

Group shots at picket line. The men are not marching now, but standing in groups on the road. Kalinsky is among them, on crutches, his leg in a cast. Ramón takes a sheet of paper from his shirt pocket and checks it.

Ramón: Now let's see... who's missing? Prieto, Sebastian. Prieto?
Second miner: Haven't seen him for two days.
Jenkins *(entering scene, grinning):* Hey, Ramón—listen to this. The chief foreman come to me last night, said he'd make me shift foreman if I'd start a back-to-work movement. "Jenkins," he says, "why string along with them tamale eaters?" I just told him I come to like tamales fine.

The men laugh, Ramón smiles, but the look he gives Jenkins is tinged with speculative suspicion. Just then a patrol of three miners led by Alfredo Díaz enters scene from the hillslope. Alfredo reports to Ramón. He is breathing hard.

Alfredo: Two scabs got through on the other side of the hill. We chased the rest back.
Ramón: Recognize them?
Alfredo *(shaking head):* Anglos. From out of town. But they're not miners—I could tell that. They don't know zinc from Shinola.
Ramón: Okay. Take five. Get yourself some coffee.

As the three men of the patrol walk off to the coffee shack, one of the miners on the picket line calls out:

First Miner: Hey, Ramón, here comes the super...

Ext., winding road. Long shot: pickets' angle. On the road from Zinc Town, across the trestle, we see a shiny new Cadillac crawling along the dusty road. It draws to a stop some distance away.

Close shot: Cadillac. Superintendent Alexander sits at the wheel. Beside him is George Hartwell, a company representative from New York. Hartwell is impeccably dressed in a gabardine suit and Panama hat. He peers over Alexander's shoulder as the superintendent points out:

> **Alexander:** You can get the best view of the layout from here. That's their main picket line. They have another post on the back road, and roving patrols...

Reverse panning shot: their angle, showing the Sheriff's cars, the picket line, the unfenced hill and the mountain of waste beyond it.

> **Hartwell's voice:** On company property? Why don't you have them thrown off?
> **Alexander's voice:** But it's all company property, Mr. Hartwell— the stores, the housing area, everything. Where do you throw them. And who does the throwing?

Alexander nods, shifts the car into gear, and they move off.

Ext., road. Medium long shot: the moving Cadillac. It makes the bend, comes on up the hill and stops again near the Sheriff's cars, which are parked some thirty paces from the picket line. The Sheriff walks toward the Cadillac.

Close shot: Cadillac, as the Sheriff comes up to Alexander's side of the car. The Sheriff has the appearance and speech of a New Mexican rancher, which he is. He touches his Stetson in a gesture of respect.

> **Sheriff:** Mornin'.
> **Alexander:** How's it going?
> **Sheriff:** Well, those new fellows you hired from out of town—we brought 'em up here in a truck this morning, but they took one look at that picket line and turned tail.
> **Hartwell** (looking at pickets): They don't look so rough to me.
> **Sheriff** (skeptically): Well, Mr. Hartwell, they've got some pretty tough hombres, 'specially that picket captain there—what's his name...Ray, Raymond something-or-other...
> **Alexander:** Oh yes. I know that one.

He shifts into gear and drives off. The Sheriff touches his Stetson courteously.

Back to picket line. The men are marching now, moving in a tight ellipse across the road. Kalinsky hobbles along beside them on his crutches. Ramón stands in the middle of the road, facing the picket line, his back to the approaching Cadillac. He lectures the men with mock severity.

> **Ramón:** Now why don't you let these gentlemen pass? Don't you know who's in that car?
>
> **Antonio** (shouting): It's the paymaster from Moscow—with our gold.
>
> **Ramón:** No, no, it's the president of the company himself—come all the way out here to make Jenkins general manager. So why you acting so mean?

The miners grin as they march, one of them slapping Jenkins on the back.

Int., Cadillac. Two shot, through windshield. The car is halted again, and the picket line can be seen in b.g. Alexander is used to this treatment, but Hartwell is annoyed.

> **Hartwell:** Aren't they going to let us pass?
>
> **Alexander:** Eventually. This is just a little ritual to impress us with their power.
>
> **Hartwell:** Childish.
>
> **Alexander:** Well, they're like children in many ways. Sometimes you have to humor them, sometimes you have to spank them—and sometimes you have to take their food away. (Points off scene.) Here comes the one we were talking about.

We see Ramón leave the picket line and come toward the car. He is still sipping his coffee. Alexander chuckles.

> **Alexander:** He's quite a character. Claims his grandfather once owned the land where the mine is now. (Both men laugh.)

Another angle: at car, Ramón comes up. He leans down and peers inside.

> **Ramón** (politely): Want to go up to your office, Mr. Alexander?
>
> **Alexander** (a half-smile): Naturally. You think I parked here for a cup of coffee?
>
> **Ramón:** You're welcome to one.
>
> **Alexander:** No thanks.
>
> **Ramón** (glancing at Hartwell): The men would like to know who this gentlemen is.
>
> **Alexander:** That's none of their affair.

Hartwell *(quickly)*: That's all right—it's no secret. My name's Hartwell. I'm from the company's Eastern office.

Ramón: You mean Delaware?

Hartwell: No. New York.

Ramón *(with mock awe)*: New York? You're not the Company President by any chance?

Hartwell *(smiles faintly)*: No.

Ramón: Too bad. The men've always wanted to get a look at the President. *(Eagerly)* But you've come out here to settle the strike?

Hartwell *(shrugging)*: Well, if that's possible . . .

Ramón: It's possible. Just negotiate.

Hartwell *(coolly, to Alexander)*: Are we talking to a union spokesman?

Alexander: Not exactly. But I wish he were one. He knows more about mining than those pie-cards we've had to deal with.

Hartwell is unprepared for Alexander's gambit—but a mask falls suddenly over Ramón's face. Alexander looks at Ramón, continuing with all the sincerity he can muster.

Alexander: I mean it. I know your work record. You were in line for foreman when this trouble started—did you know that? You had a real future with this company, but you let those Reds stir you up. And now they'll sell you down the river. Why don't you wake up, Ray? *(A pause)* That's your name, isn't it, Ray?

Ramón: No. My name is Quintero. Mister Quintero.

There is a moment of silence. Alexander compresses his lips, chagrined at the rebuff.

Alexander: Are you going to let us pass—or do I have to call the Sheriff?

Ramón: There's nothing stopping you. *(He steps back, indicating)*

The road, from their angle. The road is clear. The pickets are no longer marching, but are lined up facing each other on both sides of the road. We hear the Cadillac accelerate. It plunges forward into scene, moves on past the pickets in a cloud of dust. Ramón comes into scene, moving toward the picket post. He bellows at the miners:

Ramón: I was wrong! They don't want Jenkins for general manager—they want *me*!

The men laugh, re-form in groups on the road.

Ext., coffee shack. Medium shot. Ramón, grinning, strolls over to Esperanza, who is standing in the doorway.

> **Ramón:** You shoulda heard that guy. What a line! I was up for foreman, he says. ¡Fíjate!

Esperanza smiles, then suddenly winces. Her hand goes to her midriff. Ramón is alarmed.

> **Ramón:** What's the matter?
> **Esperanza** (smiles again): It's nothing. Just a little catch...

She takes Estella by the hand and starts to walk down the road toward the Sheriff's cars. Ramón escorts her. Camera pans with them. Suddenly we hear from very far off a boy's voice calling:

> **Voice:** Papa! Papa!...Over here!
> **Ramón** (looking back): Is that Luís? What's he doing? Playing hookey again?

The wooded hill. Long shot from their angle. In a thicket of juniper far up the slope we can make out two boys: Luís and a comrade of the same age. They are waving their arms frantically. Ramón walks into scene in f.g., cups his hands, bellows:

> **Ramón:** Luís! Come down here!
> **Luís** (barely audible): Papa! We seen 'em! Two scabs! Over there!

Closer angle: Luís and companion.

> **Second Boy** (pointing): They're hiding in the gully. Over there!

Back to picket post. The miners are trying to spot the scabs. They mill about restlessly, all talking at once.

> **Ad libs:**
> ¿Qué dijo?
> He's spotted two scabs...
> Where?
> Over in the gully...
> Come on, let's get em...
> **Ramón** (yelling): Hold it, brothers! You—Antonio—Alfredo—Cente—you come with me. The rest stay on the line.

The four men set off at a run on the road paralleling the railroad tracks. Camera holds. Esperanza comes into scene in f.g. She calls in exasperation:

Esperanza: Luís! Luís! Come back here!

Esperanza walks on, passing through the picket line.

The hillside. Long shot, as Luís and his companion run diagonally down the slope.

The gully. Long panning shot. Two figures scramble out of the gully. They run toward the railroad track, cross it and head for the uphill road to the mine.

Long panning shot: Ramón and his men running, fanning out, trying to cut off the strike-breakers. Cente makes for the tracks. Ramón stays on the road. Antonio and Alfredo dart up the hill.

Group shot: at Sheriff's cars. The deputies have roused themselves. The Sheriff smiles, gives them a sign. Four deputies climb into a sedan and drive off.

Closer angle: the two strike-breakers running. One of them, a blond Anglo, stops suddenly, then runs back the way he came. Camera follows the other man. He reaches the road leading up through the mountain of waste to the mine.

Back to Esperanza, far behind the others, but coming on steadily, walking alone, as though in a trance.

The winding road, higher up. Antonio emerges onto the road above the strike-breaker, cutting him off.

The strike-breaker: shooting toward waste heap. He veers off the road, tries to evade his pursuers by climbing the steep pile of waste, but makes no headway in the powdery dust. Slipping, clawing, he creates a small avalanche, plunges back to the road below.

The road, near foot of waste heap. The strike-breaker comes tumbling down, scrambles to his feet, runs back toward the tracks. Camera pans with him. Cente suddenly appears, blocking his way. Then Ramón appears, trapping the strike-breaker on the railroad trestle. The two miners advance slowly toward him.

Closer angle: at trestle. The strike-breaker stands there, panting, terrified. We are close enough now to recognize him. It is Sebastian Prieto.

Reverse angle, shooting toward Ramón, who stops, stunned by this unexpected betrayal.

> **Ramón** (panting): Prieto... Sebastian Prieto...

He comes on slowly toward Sebastian. There is murder in his eyes.

> **Sebastian:** Ramón... listen... for the love of God...
> **Ramón:** You... you... I'd expect it of an Anglo, yes... but you...
> **Sebastian:** Ramón... listen to me... I'm in a jam... I had to get a job...
> **Ramón:** You Judas... bloodsucker...
> **Sebastian:** Ramón—listen... my kids...
> **Ramón** (seizing his collar): ¡Tú! ¡Traidor a tu gente! ¡Rompehuelga! ¡Desgraciado!
> **Sebastian:** My kids don't have enough to eat!
> **Ramón:** (shaking him): You think my kids have enough to eat, you rat?
> **Sebastian:** I know, it's wrong. Just let me go. I'll leave town... just let me go.
> **Ramón:** (contemptuously): You think I was going to work you over? I wouldn't dirty my hands with you...

He spits in the man's face and shoves him away. Sebastian trips on the railroad track and falls.

Medium long shot: the trestle, as seen from the road. The Sheriff's car plunges into scene in f.g., skids to a stop. The deputies pile out, run toward the trestle. In the distance we see Sebastian scramble to his feet, cross the railroad spur and retreat to the gully out of which he came. Ramón stands watching him. The deputies are almost on him before he turns. One of them seizes him by the arm. He appears to be protesting but the men are out of ear-shot. Suddenly we see the flash of handcuffs snapped on Ramón's right wrist. Ramón, offering no resistance, holds up his left hand—but a deputy spins him around with an armlock and snaps Ramón's wrists together behind his back. It all happens very quickly, and they lead him off.

Another angle, featuring miners and boys standing in a group now, watching the arrest. Luís starts to run to his father, but Antonio holds him back.

Medium shot: at Sheriff's car. Ramón is thrust roughly into the back seat of the car between two deputies. The other two get in front. The driver turns the car around, raising a great cloud of dust. The car speeds off. Camera pans with it, holds on Esperanza watching at the side of the road. Suddenly Esperanza winces. her hands go to her belly, and she bends slightly, as though from a severe cramp.

Close shot: Esperanza. Her face contorted with pain, with the realization that her labor has begun. She looks around helplessly, calls:

> **Esperanza:** Luís! Luís! The baby...

Medium long shot from her angle: Luís and men listening, paralyzed, as we hear in Spanish:

> **Esperanza's voice:** The baby! Get the women! Quick!

Ext., back road. Medium long shot. The Sheriff's car speeds toward us down the road, stops suddenly in a swirl of dust. This is an isolated area near the mine; no observers can be seen.

Int., back seat of Sheriff's car. Medium close shot. Ramón sits very straight, his wrists locked behind his back. The deputy on his left is a freckled-face youth named Kimbrough. The deputy on his right is a pale, cavernous, slack-jawed man named Vance. Vance is slowly drawing on a pigskin glove. Ramón glances at the glove. Then he looks out the window.

> **Ramón** (his voice low, tremulous): Why do you stop?
> **Kimbrough** (grins): Wanna have a talk with you—'bout why you slugged that fellow back there.
> **Ramón:** That's a lie. I didn't—

The gloved hand comes up, swipes Ramón across the mouth.

> **Vance** (softly): Now you know that ain't no way to talk to a white man.

Ext., road, near picket post. Medium long shot. We can see Mrs. Salazar and several other women running to meet Esperanza. A couple of pickets follow along. Mrs. Salazar shouts back at them in Spanish:

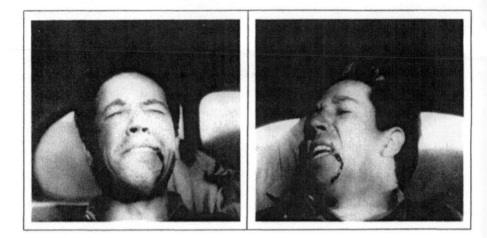

Mrs. Salazar: Go back and get a blanket, you idiots! So we can carry her!

Int., Sheriff's car. Medium full shot. Ramón sits tense now, awaiting the next blow. A trickle of blood runs down his chin. The two deputies in front sit like wax dummies, paying no attention to what is going on in back.

> **Kimbrough:** Hey, Vance. You said this bull-fighter was full of pepper. He don't look so peppery now.
> **Vance:** Oh, but he is. He's full of chili, this boy.

He drives a gloved fist into Ramón's belly. Ramón gasps, his eyes bulge.

> **Vance:** He likes it hot. His chiquita makes it good and hot for him —don't she, Pancho?

Vance strikes him in the abdomen again. Kimbrough snickers.

Ext., road; another Sheriff's car near picket line. Medium shot. The Sheriff is standing there with his other two deputies when Kalinsky hobbles up.

> **Kalinsky** *(breathlessly):* Sheriff...we need a doctor—quick. A lady's gonna have a baby...
> **Sheriff:** What d'ya take me for? An ambulance driver?
> **Kalinsky:** But there's a company doctor in town. We don't have a car. If you'd just go get him...

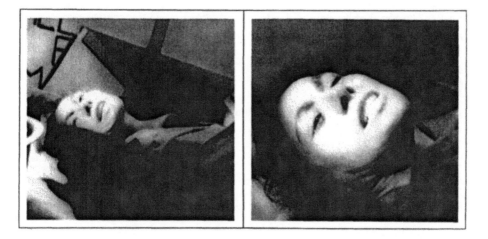

Sheriff: You kiddin'? Company doctor won't come to no picket line.

Kalinsky clenches his fists, furious, helpless. Then he labors back toward the coffee shack. Camera pans with him. In the distance we see four men carrying Esperanza on a folded blanket.

Ext., coffee shack. Full shot. Mrs. Salazar is walking beside the improvised stretcher. She directs the men to enter the shack.

Mrs. Salazar: We can't get her home...there isn't time. Take her inside...

Int., Sheriff's car. Close shot. Ramón is doubled up, his head between his legs. Vance pulls him erect.

Vance: Hold your head up, Pancho. That ain't no way to sit.
Ramón *(a mutter in Spanish):* I'll outlive you all, you lice.
Vance *(softly):* How's that? What's that Spic talk?

He strikes Ramón in the belly. Ramón gives a choked cry.

Now the intercutting becomes very rapid. The shots are brief flashes. Close-up: Esperanza lying on a cot in the coffee shack, her face contorted with pain. She gasps:

Esperanza: God forgive me...wishing...this child would never be born.

39

Back to Ramón. Kimbrough holds up Ramón's head while Vance punches him methodically. Ramón gasps in Spanish:

Ramón: Mother of God... have mercy...

Close-up: Esperanza.

Esperanza *(in Spanish):* Have mercy on this child... let this child live...

Close-up: Ramón biting his lip in agony.

Ramón *(in Spanish):* Oh, my God... Esperanza... Esperanza...

Ramón's voice carries over to close-up: Esperanza.

Esperanza: Ramón...

A contraction seizes her and she screams, her scream carrying over.

Close-up: Ramón. Now the two images merge, and undulate, and blur, as with receding consciousness. And then darkness on the screen. We hear the feeble wail of a newborn infant.

Dissolve to: int., Catholic church. Full shot, day. Except for the altar lights in deep b.g. the church is in shadow. A group of five men and five women are silhouetted at the altar rail, facing the priest. We cannot immediately identify them.

Esperanza's voice: Ramón was in the hospital for a week... and then in the county jail for thirty days... charged with assault and resisting arrest. But I made up my mind to postpone the christening till he could be there....

Group shot: at altar rail, including not only the Quintero family but also Antonio and Luz, Teresa and Charley, Ruth and Frank, Sal and Consuelo. Antonio holds the baby up to the priest, who makes the sign of the cross. His lips move in prayer. Ramón peers fondly at the baby over Antonio's shoulder.

Esperanza's voice: ... And so the baby was baptized the day Ramón got out of jail. Antonio was his godfather, and Teresa was his godmother. We christened him Juan.

The priest sprinkles holy water over the infant's head.

Wipe to: int., Quintero cottage: parlor. Full shot, night. The same men are seated around the parlor table, playing poker. From the phonograph we hear Mexican dance music. Consuelo bustles in with coffee for the men.

> **Esperanza's voice:** That night we had a double celebration: Juanito's christening, Ramón's homecoming.

Int., bedroom. Full shot: The room is almost completely dark but we can make out the forms of six children sleeping crossways on the bed. The baby's crib is beside the bed.

> **Esperanza's voice:** And we put all the children to sleep in the bedroom, as usual. . . .

Int., kichen. Full shot. The five wives are gathered there, preparing sandwiches, talking.

> **Esperanza's voice:** And the ladies adjourned to the kitchen—as usual.

Int., parlor: at poker table. Camera angle is that of a standing kibitzer. Ramón is nearest the kitchen. Around him clockwise sit Antonio, Sal, Charley and Frank. Sal is dealing the fifth card of a stud poker hand. The play is continuous and fast, a counterpoint to the more serious discussion.

> **Esperanza's voice:** And the men took over the parlor—as usual.

Her voice fades, and now we hear:

> **Charley** (throwing in matches): Five thousand dollars.
> **Frank:** Beats.
> **Antonio:** Raise you ten thousand.
> **Charley:** You dog. All right, let's see them.
> **Antonio:** Aces, wired. (Scooping up pile of matches.) Come to papa.

While Charley gathers the cards and shuffles, Frank turns to Ramón.

> **Ramón:** Hear those deputies slugged Cente.
> **Frank:** Yeah. Lots of provocation lately. They figure if they can lock up the leadership on some phony riot charge, maybe they can bust the strike.

Int., kitchen. Full shot, as Teresa reenters from the parlor. Ruth Barnes is tapping her foot restlessly to the radio music which continues over scene.

> **Ruth:** Are we gonna let them play poker all night? I want to dance.
> **Luz** *(roguishly):* With whose husband?
> **Ruth:** With any of them—even my own.
> **Luz:** If you dance with my husband, you'll have to put up with this. . .

She grabs Ruth and dances her around in a lascivious parody of Antonio's style. The women giggle. Esperanza's head turns at the sound of an infant's wail.

Int., parlor: At the poker table. Frank is shuffling the cards. Esperanza is seen crossing the bedroom in b.g.

> **Sal** *(to Ramón):* And another thing. Your attitude toward Anglos. If you're gonna be a leader . . .
> **Ramón** *(cutting in):* What attitude?
> **Sal:** You lump them all together—Anglo workers and Anglo bosses.
> **Ramón** *(indicating Frank):* He's a guest in my house, isn't he?
> **Sal:** Sure. But you want the truth? You're even suspicious of him.
> **Ramón:** Maybe. I think he's got a few things to learn about our people.

There is a rather uneasy pause. Esperanza is seen recrossing from bedroom to kitchen, the baby in her arms. Frank continues shuffling.

> **Frank:** Go on. Spill it.
> **Ramón** *(slowly):* Well, you're the organizer. You work out strike strategy—and most of the time you're dead right. But when you figure everything the rank-and-file's to do, down to the last detail, you don't give *us* anything to think about. You afraid we're too lazy to take initiative?
> **Frank** *(defensively):* You know I don't think that.
> **Ramón:** Maybe not. But there's another thing . . . like when you came in tonight—*(indicates picture)* I heard you ask your wife, "Who's that? His grandfather?"

Close shot: portrait of Juárez.

Ramón's voice: That's Juárez—the father of Mexico. If I didn't know a picture of George Washington, you'd say I was an awful dumb Mexican.

Back to group.

Charley (*softening the blow*): I've never seen it fail. Try to give Ramón a friendly criticism and he throws it right back in your face.
Frank: No. He's right. I've got a lot to learn.
Antonio: Now we've got that settled, deal the cards.

Frank deals. Sal grins at Frank.

Sal: If it makes you feel any better, he's got even less use for women.

Back to kitchen. Full shot. Esperanza sits on a stool near the stove, her back to Camera and the other women, nursing the baby. Teresa and Consuelo are sampling the sandwiches they have made.

Consuelo: What are they talking about in there?
Ruth (*from the doorway*): Discussing each other's weaknesses.
Luz (*mock surprise*): I didn't know they had any.
Ruth (*looking o.s.*): Right now, Ramón's on the receiving end.
Teresa: Let's break up that game.

Back to men at poker table.

Frank (*earnestly to Ramón*): If the women are shut off from life in the union...
Antonio: Bet your hand!

Ruth enters scene with coffee for the men. The other women, save Esperanza, trail in behind her. Frank is so intent on his point that he ignores Ruth's presence.

Frank: We can't think of them just as housewives—but as allies. And we've got to treat them as such.
Ruth (*snorts*): Look who's talking! The Great White Father, and World's Champion of Women's Rights.
Frank: Aw, cut it out, Ruth.
Ruth (*to Ramón*): Me, I'm a camp follower—following this organizer from one mining camp to another—Montana, Colorado,

Idaho. But did he ever think to organize the women? No. Wives don't count in the Anglo locals either.

Ramón laughs. Ruth turns back to him.

> **Ruth:** Not that I like the way you treat your wife. But when Doctor Barnes gives you his cure-all for female troubles, ask him if he's tried it at home.
> **Ramón** (grinning): Hey, Esperanza!
> **Ruth:** Esperanza's nursing the baby.

A glow of eagerness brightens Ramón's face. He flings down the cards and goes out to the kitchen. The exasperated Antonio tosses his cards aside.

> **Antonio:** There goes the game.
> **Luz:** Good. Consuelo, turn up the radio. (To Antonio) Come on, Papa, on your feet.

Antonio gets up and begins to dance with his wife. We mark how accurate a parody his wife made of his style. Charley dances with Teresa. Ruth folds her arms, glaring at Frank.

Int., kitchen. Close two shot. Ramón stands beside his wife, looking over her shoulder at the suckling child. Camera angle is such that we cannot see Juanito.

> **Ramón** (proudly): Look at him...

Ramón clenches his fists, tenses his forearms, grunts approvingly.

> **Ramón:** A fighter, huh?
> **Esperanza:** He was born fighting. And born hungry.
> **Ramón:** Drink, drink, Juanito. You'll never have it so good.
> **Esperanza:** He'll have it good. Some day.

For a moment they say nothing, watching the baby. Then, with a side-long worried glance:

> **Esperanza:** What were they saying? About you? In there?
> **Ramón:** They say I am no good to you.
> **Esperanza** (shrugs): You are no good to me—in jail.
> **Ramón** (musing): I'd lie on my cot in the cell and I couldn't sleep with the bugs and the stink and the heat. And I'd say to myself,

think of something nice. Something beautiful. And then I'd think of you. And my heart would pound against the cot for love of you.

Esperanza is deeply moved, but she does not show him her face. Ramón's face becomes tense with determination.

> **Ramón** *(half-whispering):* Not just Juanito. You'll have it good too, Esperanza. We're going to win this strike.
> **Esperanza:** What makes you so sure?
> **Ramón** *(brooding):* Because if we lose, we lose more than a strike. We lose the union. And the men know this. And if we win, we win more than a few demands. We win... *(groping for words)* something bigger. Hope. Hope for our kids. Juanito can't grow strong on milk alone.

His words are shattered by a loud knock at the front door. Ramón turns, listening. We hear the door open and voices indistinctly. Camera holds on Ramón and Esperanza.

> **Voices:**
> This the Quintero place?
> What do you want?
> Got a court order...
> You don't get in here without a warrant.
> We got the warrant too...
> We don't want no trouble. All we want's the radio.

Ramón goes abruptly. Camera holds on Esperanza, listening.

> **Kimbrough's voice:** We don't like to break in on you like this, but this fella owns the radio store, he got himself a repossession order on this radio here.
> **Ramón's voice:** Don't touch it.
> **Kimbrough's voice:** I don't want no trouble, Quintero. We got orders to repossess this machine.

Esperanza rises swiftly, moves toward the parlor with the baby.

> **Ramón's voice:** I said... don't touch it.

Int., parlor. Full shot. Everyone is standing. Several armed deputies stand around the radio console, ready to move it, but checked momentarily by Ramón. Kimbrough's right hand is on the butt of his revolver. Esperanza enters scene. In one continuous movement, she hands the baby to Consuelo and blocks Ramón, clutching him, and speaking with a new-found fierceness.

> **Esperanza:** Let them take it!
> **Ramón:** Over my dead body.
> **Esperanza:** I don't want your dead body. I don't want you back in jail either.
> **Ramón:** But it's *yours.* I won't let them . . .
> **Esperanza** (*savagely, in Spanish*): Can't you see they want to start a fight so that they can lock you *all* up at one time?

Slowly, Ramón goes lax, and Esperanza relaxes her hold on him. The deputies pick up the heavy console, lug it toward the front door. The Quinteros' guests are glum and silent. The deputies leave, closing the door behind them.

> **Ramón** (*bitterly*): What are you so sad about?

He crosses to a shelf, picks up a dusty guitar and tosses it to Sal.

> **Ramón:** Let's hear some real music for a change.

Sal grins. He begins to improvise as we Dissolve to: Ext., mine and picket post. Long panoramic shot, day. In the distance we can see the tiny figures of the strikers maintaining their vigil on the picket line. Behind them looms the lifeless head frame of the mine.

> **Esperanza's voice:** But the strike did not end. Ramón was wrong. It went on and on, into the fourth month, the fifth, the sixth. The company still refused to negotiate. We couldn't buy food at the company store. . . .

Ext., store window. Medium close shot, day. A Mexican-American woman is looking at a display of canned foods in the window of a small town store. We see a hand place a small placard in the store window. It reads: NO CREDIT TO STRIKERS. Camera moves in till the sign fills the screen, and we wipe to:

> **Esperanza's voice:** They tried to turn people against us. They printed lies about us in their newspapers. . . .

The picket line. Medium shot, day. A dozen or so pickets march counterclockwise in a leisurely fashion. Antonio holds an unfolded newspaper which he appears to be reading to the others, but we hear:

> **Esperanza's voice:** They tried to turn the Anglo miners against us. They said that all the Mexicans ought to be sent back where they came from. But the men said . . .

Esperanza's voice fades, and now we hear from the picket line:

> **Antonio** *(slapping newspaper):* How can I go back where I came from? The shack I was born in is buried under company property.
> **Kalinsky:** Why don't nobody ever tell the bosses to go back where they came from?
> **Cente:** Wouldn't be no bosses in the state of New Mexico if they did.
> **Alfredo** *(dreamily):* Brother! Live to see the day.
> **Antonio:** Jenkins ain't no boss. *(Winking)* Mean we're gonna let people like Jenkins stay here?
> **Ramón:** You can't send him back to Oklahoma. It'd be inhumane.
> **Jenkins** *(grinning):* But I was born in Texas.
> **Antonio and Alfredo** *(mock horror):* Oh *no.* That's even worse.

They all start laughing, pummelling Jenkins as they march.

Wipe to: an ancient jalopy. Full shot, day, on a dirt road outside an adobe house. The car is piled high with the belongings of a Mexican-American family. The mother and her children are in the car. The man is shaking hands with the neighbors in a sad goodbye.

> **Esperanza's voice:** And the seventh month came. By now the strike fund was nearly gone. A few families couldn't take it any longer. They packed up and moved away—and where they went we do not know . . .

Int., union hall. Medium shot at desk, day. Sal and Charley are seated behind the desk. A number of miners stand opposite them. One by one, the miners count out money, hand it to the union officers. Ramón stands nearby, watching.

> **Esperanza's voice:** And so it was decided by the union that hardship cases should seek work in other mines. And this was done.

And the strikers who found jobs divided their pay with the union, so the rest of us might eat.

Int., Quintero cottage. Medium shot, evening. The Quintero family is seated at the table. Their plates are empty. Esperanza picks up a bowl containing two spoonfuls of beans. She divides them among the children.

> **Esperanza's voice:** Ramón was not a hardship case. Only three children to feed. No—the Quintero family was not hungry all the time. Just most of the time.

Ext., union hall. Full shot: a truck, day. Two men stand in the back of the truck, handing down cases of food to the miners. One of the men in the truck is a Negro. When Charley Vidal comes over, the Negro leans down and shakes his hand warmly.

> **Esperanza's voice:** Even so, the mine owners might have starved us out were it not for the help we got from our International in Denver, and from the other locals....And we who thought no one outside our county knew of our troubles, or cared if they did know—found we were wrong.

Int., union hall. Close shot at desk, day. The desk is piled high with mail. Sal and Frank are opening it. We see dollar bills, loose change, checks.

> **Esperanza's voice:** Letters came. From our own people, the Spanish-speaking people of the Southwest...and from far away —Butte, Chicago, Birmingham, New York—messages of solidarity and the crumpled dollar bills of working men.

Camera pulls back slowly to disclose two women at a mimeograph machine.

Camera pans slowly around the union hall, disclosing other women at work—cutting stencils, filing papers, sealing envelopes, etc. Several small children romp and climb over the benches.

> **Esperanza's voice:** But that was not all—we women were helping. And not just as cooks and coffee makers. A few of the men made jokes about it, but the work had to be done—so they let us stay.

Medium shot, featuring Esperanza standing behind a desk, sealing envelopes. The infant Juanito lies on an improvised pallet beside her, hemmed in by piles of leaflets. Estella is licking stamps.

Esperanza's voice: No one knew how great a change it was, till the day of the crisis...

Full shot: the union hall. The Sheriff, a U.S. Marshal and several deputies appear suddenly in the entrance to the hall. They cross the room to Sal Ruíz' desk. The Sheriff is grinning broadly.

Esperanza's voice: That was the day when the Sheriff and the Marshal came. The Sheriff was smiling—so we knew he brought bad news.

Closer angle: group at table. Sal takes the paper, reads it gravely. The Sheriff grins triumphantly and leaves, followed by his entourage.

Esperanza's voice: The company had got a court injunction ordering the strikers to stop picketing. A Taft-Hartley injunction, they called it. It meant heavy fines and jail sentences for the strikers if they disobeyed.

Sal rises slowly, re-reading the court order as Frank and Charley join him, reading over his shoulder. Their faces express worry, defeat.

Esperanza's voice: A decision had to be made at once—whether to obey the order, or not.

Wipe to: Int., union hall. Full panning shot, night. The hall is packed. The striking miners, as usual, occupy the center bloc of seats. But this time there are almost as many women as men in the hall. They sit with their children in the rear or on benches against the side walls.

Camera holds on Frank Barnes, standing at the front of the hall, addressing the miners.

Frank *(as Esperanza's voice fades):* If we obey the court, the strike will be lost...the scabs would move in as soon as the pickets disappear. If we defy the court, the pickets will be arrested and the strike will be lost anyway.

Closer angle, featuring Frank.

Frank: So there it is brothers. The bosses have us coming and going. I just want to say this—no matter which way you decide, the International will back you up—as it's always backed you up. This is a democratic union. The decision's up to you.

Reverse angle, shooting past Frank at miners. We hear a rumble of dissatisfaction as Frank sits down. There is no applause. Heads huddling, the miners grapple with the dilemma. Ramón rises angrily.

> **Ramón:** If we give up now, if we obey this rotten Taft-Hartley law, we give up everything it's taken us fifty years to gain. There is only one answer: fight them! Fight them all!
> **Other miners:**
> How?
> They'll arrest us!
> We gain nothing.

Their voices fade. Ramón, still on his feet, turns on his critics, lashing them. Another miner rises, extending his arms in a gesture of helplessness. Over this we hear:

> **Esperanza's voice:** The men quarreled. They made brave speeches. It seemed that Brother Barnes was right—the company had them coming and going. It seemed the strike was lost.

Full shot: the union hall. Another angle. In near f.g. Chairman Ruíz is on his feet, pounding his gavel. In b.g. we can see Teresa Vidal waving for recognition. The chair recognizes her. Teresa has advanced to the speakers' table in f.g. Though obviously scared, she is not as inarticulate or halting as Consuelo had been.

> **Teresa:** Brother Chairman, if you read the court injunction carefully you will see that it only prohibits *striking miners* from picketing. *(A pause.)* We women are not striking miners. We will take over your picket line.

We hear a stirring, then a raucous male laugh.

> **Teresa:** Don't laugh. *We* have a solution. You have none. Brother Quintero was right when he said we'll lose fifty years of gains if we lose this strike. Your wives and children too. But this we promise —if the women take your places on the picket line, the strike will *not* be broken, and no scabs will take your jobs.

There is silence in the hall now. Teresa starts to walk back to her seat when Sal's voice checks her.

> **Sal:** If that's a motion ... only members of the union can make a motion.

Sal glances at Charley Vidal, who sits beside him. Charley hesitates. Teresa glares at her husband. Charley takes a deep breath, yells:

> **Charley:** I so move!
> **Voice** *(from the floor):* Second!
> **Sal** *(uneasy):* You've heard the motion. The floor is open for debate.
> **Miner:** If we allow our *women* to help us, we'll be the joke of the whole labor movement!
> **Another miner:** Look, brother, our women are ours, our country-women! Why shouldn't they help us?

The hall. Another angle. We see miners with their heads together in heated argument, grimaces and gestures of disapproval, individual miners rising to address the chair.

Another angle, featuring Luz Morales. Eyes flashing, she addresses the men.

> **Esperanza's voice:** And Luz asked which was worse, to hide behind a woman's skirt, or go down on his knees before the boss?

Another angle, featuring Gonzales.

> **Gonzales:** We haven't counted enough on our women. The bosses haven't counted on them at all.

Another angle, featuring Charley Vidal.

> **Charley:** Will the bosses win *now* because we have no unity between the men and their wives and sisters?

Another angle, featuring a miner and his wife. A husky miner named José Sánchez can be seen goading his wife to speak. The frightened woman finally obeys.

> **Esperanza's voice:** And Carlotta Sánchez said she didn't think picketing was proper for ladies. It wasn't nice. Maybe even a sin.

Another angle, featuring Gonzales and Ramón.

> **Gonzales:** I say give the sisters a chance...

Gonzales' voice fades, and Ramón rises, glancing angrily at Gonzales, and begins to speak.

Ramón: And what will happen when the cops come, and beat our women up? Will we stand there? Watch them? No. We'll take over anyway, and we'll be right back where we are now. Only worse. Even *more* humiliated. Brothers, I beg you—don't allow this.

nón sits down. There is scattered applause from the men. Someone ; the question.

'erse angle, shooting toward chairman.

Sal *(rapping his gavel):* All right. The question's been called. You brothers know what you're voting on—that the sisters of the auxiliary take over the picket line. All those in favor will so signify . . .

Teresa's voice *(a bellow):* Brother Chairman! A point of order!

ler angle, shooting toward Teresa and Esperanza. Teresa nudges Es-anza. She rises shyly. It seems that Esperanza's stage fright will leave mute—but at last she finds her voice:

Esperanza: I don't know anything . . . about these questions of parliament. But you men are voting on something the *women* are to do, or not to do. So I think it's only fair the women be allowed to vote—especially if they have to do the job.

hear cries of approval from the women's section, intermingled with uted objections from some men.

up shot: at chairman's table. Sal has to make a ruling, but he seems lecided. He glances at Charley. Charley winks, nods. He glances at hk. Frank grins and nods. Sal clears his throat.

Sal: Brothers . . . and sisters. It would be unconstitutional to permit women to vote at a union meeting. *(Male applause.)* If there's no objection, we could adjourn this meeting . . . *(There are cries of protest from men and women alike. He holds up his hand.)* No, wait, wait . . . and reconvene this meeting as a community mass meeting with every adult entitled to a vote!

Voice: I so move!

Second voice: Second!

Sal: All those in favor will raise their hands. *(Most of the hands are raised.)* The ayes have it! Now, every adult is entitled to a vote!

Women's voices: Question! Question! Call the question!

Sal *(grinning):* Those in favor that the sisters take over the picket line will so signify by raising their hands.

The hall. Full panning shot from Sal's angle. An overwhelming majority of the women are voting for the plan. About a third of the men raise their hands—but some of them lower their arms when nudged angrily by their neighbors. Tellers move through the hall counting hands. Camera holds on Ramón, who is practically sitting on his hands. He frowns at:

Esperanza, from his angle, her eyes averted, but her hand defiantly up.

Back to chairman. The tellers approach Sal, whisper the affirmative vote. He adds the totals, then pounds his gavel.

Sal: Okay. All those opposed?

Full panning shot: as before. Most of the women sit with their fingers intertwined, as though in prayer. A few weaker sisters raise their hands uncertainly. Their neighbors nudge them. The hands come down again. Camera pans to the men as the tellers count. We see a forest of raised hands. Some miners are frantically holding up both arms.

Back to chairman. Medium shot. The tellers give Sal their figures. Sal's face is grave, reveals nothing. He rises, announces quietly:

Sal: The motion has carried—a hundred and three to eighty-five. *(No applause.)*

Reverse angle. Full panning shot. A profound stillness has settled over the hall. The men turn in their places, looking at their womenfolk with doubt, apprehension, expectancy. Camera pans to the women who line the side wall. They look at each other with a breathless wonder as the full import of their undertaking dawns on them. Fade out.

Fade in: ext., picket line. Long panoramic shot, morning. This panorama should be as sweeping a vista as the first scene of the picket line. We get the sense of women streaming toward the picket post from four points of the compass. Some arrive in ancient cars, others walk by way of the road or foot paths or the railroad tracks. There are so many women on the line that even though they march two abreast they overlap the road.

Esperanza's voice: And so they came, the women... they rose before dawn and they came, wives, daughters, grandmothers.

They came from Zinc Town and the hills beyond, from other mining camps, ten, twenty, thirty miles away...

Closer view: the picket line. The women march in an orderly, determined fashion. There is no gaiety. Teresa and Mrs. Salazar are in charge. They are as bold and self-assured as two drill sergeants. Most of the women are dressed for the occasion—wearing shirts, jeans and sneakers or saddle shoes.

Esperanza's voice: By sun-up there were a hundred on the line. And they kept coming—women we had never seen before, women who had nothing to do with the strike. Somehow they heard about a women's picket line—and they came.

Medium long shot: miners on hillside. On the steep wooded slope above the picket post the varsity squats on its collective haunches. The men smoke, watching the picket line with mingled awe and apprehension.

Esperanza's voice: And the men came too. They looked unhappy. I think they were afraid. Afraid the women wouldn't stand fast —or maybe afraid they would.

56

The hillside. Another angle, higher up the slope. Several miners stand here with their families. They, too, look unhappy. Jenkins and his wife are among them.

> **Esperanza's voice:** But not all the women went to the picket post. Some were forbidden by their husbands. *(A pause.)* I was one of these.

Close group shot: the Quintero family standing apart from the others, near a clump of junipers. Luís stands beside his father, whose uneasy frown is directed at the picket line. Estella stands beside her mother, who holds the baby Juanito in her arms. Esperanza keeps gazing at the picket line off scene, never at Ramón.

> **Esperanza:** It's not fair...I should be there with them. After all, I'm the one who got the women the vote.
> **Ramón** *(stubbornly):* No.
> **Esperanza:** But the motion passed. It's...it's not democratic of you to...
> **Ramón:** *(interrupting):* The union don't run my house. *(After a*

long pause.) Those Anglo dames stirred you up to make fools of yourselves—but you don't *see* any of *them* down there.

Esperanza *(squinting, peering):* Yes, I do. There's Ruth Barnes.

Ramón: She's the organizer's wife. She's got to be there.

Esperanza: No, she *wants* to be there. *(Looking off)* And there's Mrs. Kalinsky.

Ramón *(pointing off scene):* There's Jenkins's wife. You don't see her on no picket line.

Esperanza *(quietly):* Anglo husbands can also be backward.

Ramón: Can be *what?*

Esperanza: Backward.

He glances quizzically at her. She keeps staring at:

The picket line from their angle.

> **Esperanza's voice** *(plaintively):* Can't I even put in an appearance?
>
> **Ramón's voice:** In heaven's name, woman, with a baby in your arms?

Back to family group.

> **Esperanza:** The baby likes to be walked. It helps him burp.

Ramón shakes his head. He looks off at:

The Sheriff's convoy. Long shot. Some fifty paces beyond the picket line we can see two open trucks and two Sheriff's cars. The trucks are loaded with men.

Ext., Sheriff's car. Medium shot. Superintendent Alexander, Chief Foreman Barton, the Sheriff and the deputy Vance are standing beside the car. Alexander is in a petulant mood, but the Sheriff and Vance seem amused by the situation. Three pretty Mexican-American girls pass by on their way to the picket line. Vance whistles at them. As they move out of the scene Vance calls:

> **Vance:** Hey, girls! Wait a minute! Don't you wanta see my pistol?
>
> **Alexander:** Shut up. *(As the Sheriff chuckles.)* What's so amusing? They're flaunting a court order.
>
> **Sheriff** *(grins):* Not so sure about that. Letter of the Law, you know. All the injunction says is no picketing by miners.
>
> **Alexander** *(furious):* Whose side are you on anyway?

Sheriff: Now don't get excited, Mr. Alexander. They'll scatter like a covey of quail.

Barton *(impatiently):* Well, let's get at it—before another hundred dames show up.

Sheriff *(rouses himself, calls):* All right, boys.

Wider angle: the convoy. Drivers and deputies climb into the cabs of each truck. Barton, Vance and two other deputies get into the lead car. Vance holds up his tear gas gun.

Vance: What about these?

Sheriff: Forget it. They'll scatter like quail.

Barton starts the motor. He waves at the truck drivers and the other Sheriff's car. They wave back. The convoy starts up, gathering speed rapidly.

Full shot: miners on the hillslope. They spring to their feet, tense.

Full shot: the picket line. The women stop marching, turn in unison to face the oncoming convoy.

Full panning shot: the convoy hurtling toward the picket line.

Close shot: faces of miners. They groan involuntarily.

Close shot: faces of women pickets, steady, unflinching.

The Sheriff's car from their angle, horn blowing, speeding directly at them, looming bigger, closer.

Full shot: the picket line. At the last split second, Barton jams on his brakes, and the car skids. The women have not moved.

Close shot: women and car. The car skids into the picket line. A woman is swiped by the front fender, flung onto the road.

Full shot: the picket line. We hear a collective gasp from the women. Then they scream. Two women run to their injured sister. The others swarm around the car. The deputies are trying to get the doors open. The women begin to rock the car. Finally the deputies manage to get out. They flail the women with their fists, their gun stocks. But there are four women to each deputy, and they cling to the men, grabbing at their weapons.

Medium shot: the first truck. The Anglo scabs standing in the back of the truck react in fear and consternation. But they stay where they are.

Medium long shot: miners on hillside. A group of them start coming down the hill. We can see Charley and Frank gesturing, trying to restrain them—but the miners come on.

Back to the picket post. Vance kicks out at woman who is trying to tear off his cartridge-belt, sends her sprawling. He backs off, panic-stricken, and fires a tear gas shell into a mass of women pickets. The exploding shell disperses them momentarily. The women fan out, coughing and choking.

The picket post, shooting from hill above. At Mrs. Salazar's command, the women form into two platoons; the larger group remains on the road, blocking the convoy, despite the fact that other deputies open fire with tear gas; but another line has formed at the side of the road, facing the miners bent on entering the fray.

Closer angle: the second picket line. As the miners coming down the slope reach the road, Mrs. Salazar waves them back angrily, yells in Spanish:

> **Mrs. Salazar:** Get back! Get back! Stay out of this!
> **First miner** (desperately): But they're beating up my wife!
> **Women** (simultaneously in English and Spanish):
> It'll be worse if you get in it.
> Then they'll start shooting...
> They'll throw you in jail!
> We can take care of ourselves...
> You're not needed here...
> Get back! Get back!

The men fall back, nonplussed by the vehemence of the women.

Back to picket post. Long shot from hillside. Other deputies have come running from the rear of the convoy to support the four outnumbered deputies. The scabs remain in their trucks. But the wind is blowing the wrong way, and the tear gas drifts back toward the trucks. The scabs begin to cough. A couple of them jump over the tailgate of the first truck and run. That starts a panicky rout. Other scabs tumble out of the trucks and run back down the road to escape the tear gas.

Close group shot: the Quintero family staring at the action. Esperanza can't stand it any longer. She hands the baby to Ramón and is gone before he realizes her intent.

His view: Esperanza running diagonally down the slope toward the picket post. In the distance we see deputies still battling the women. The deputies seem to have lost their heads. They lash out viciously at any woman who confronts them, in a vain attempt to scatter the women and clear the road.

Closer angle: the picket post. Luz Morales is climbing Vance's back, clinging to his arms. Another woman clutches at his gun hand, trying to prevent him from drawing his pistol. Esperanza comes running up. She stops for a second, slips off her right shoe. Vance knocks the other woman down, pulls his revolver from his holster. Esperanza whacks him over the wrist with her shoe, knocking the weapon out of his hand. Luz digs into his hair with both hands.

Back to Ramón on hillside, helpless, speechless, holding the baby. Suddenly he runs out of scene. Luís grabs Estella's hand, follows.

Another part of the hill: the lower slope. Charley and Frank are watching the action. Ramón comes running into scene.

> **Ramón:** Why are you standing there? Do something!
> **Charley** (looking o.s.): Relax.
> **Ramón:** But women are getting hurt! We've gotta take over!
> **Charley:** They're doing all right.
> **Frank** (grins, looks at baby): Anyway, looks like you've got your hands full.

Completely frustrated, Ramón looks down at the tiny bundle in his arms. Then he looks off at:

The picket post: long shot from Ramón's angle. We can see Barton calling his men off. He jumps in the car, turns it around. Several deputies climb aboard as he drives off. The others retreat on foot, leaving the two abandoned trucks. The women re-form their lines, and begin to sing "The Union Is Our Leader."

Dissolve to: int., Quintero cottage. Full shot: parlor, late afternoon. Ramón paces the floor fretfully, puffing on a cigarette. The baby crib is in a corner, and Juanito is wailing. Estella tries to match her father's caged-lion stride.

> **Estella:** Papa, I'm hungry.
> **Ramón** *(a growl):* So'm I.

Luís enters from the front door. Ramón glares at him.

> **Ramón:** Where's your mama?
> **Luís:** She's coming. Charley Vidal gave her a lift.

The boy starts off, then turns back again, his eyes glowing.

> **Luís:** Boy! Did you see the way Mama whopped that deputy with her shoe? Knocked the gun right out...
> **Ramón** *(thundering):* I don't want you hanging around there, hear?

We hear the sound of a chugging truck outside. Ramón goes to the window, peers out.

Ext., road outside Quintero cottage. Medium shot. The union pick-up, full of women, stops at the gate. Esperanza and Luz sit beside Charley in the cab. They get out. All the women are laughing and smiling.

Int., parlor. Full shot, as Esperanza enters. She is dirty, bedraggled, and bone-tired—but there is a new light in her eyes, and when she smiles she grins.

> **Ramón** *(hoping for the worst):* You all right?
> **Esperanza:** Sure.

She kisses him lightly on the cheek, kisses Estella and Luís, crosses immediately to the crib, glances at Juanito and enters the kitchen. Camera pans with her. Ramón follows slowly, halts in the kitchen doorway.

> **Ramón:** Must've been some experience for you, huh?
> **Esperanza** *(from kitchen):* Yes.
> **Ramón:** I guess you got enough today to last a lifetime, huh?
> **Esperanza** *(from kitchen):* I'm going back tomorrow.

She emerges from the kitchen with the baby's bottle, crosses to the crib. The infant's wailing ceases abruptly. Ramón comes over, scowling.

> **Ramón:** You might get hurt. *(No response.)* Listen, if you think

I'm gonna play nursemaid from now on, you're crazy...I've had these kids all day!

Esperanza *(simply):* I've had them since the day they were born.

She exits to the kitchen. Ramón trails after her.

Int., kitchen. Medium shot. Esperanza works swiftly, putting pots and pans on the stove, preparing supper, etc. Ramón continues to scowl at her.

Ramón: I'm telling you. I don't stay home with these kids tomorrow.

Esperanza *(calmly):* Okay. Then, tomorrow, I take the kids with me to the picket line.

Dissolve to: ext., picket line. Full panning shot, day. There are fewer women on the line than on the first day, but they march with the same assurance and discipline as before. A good half of them crochet as they march.

Esperanza's voice: And so I came back the next day—and every day for the next month...

Camera pans past the picket line to the coffee shack, moves on to pick up a group of small children playing near the road.

Esperanza's voice: I kept Juanito in the coffee shack, and when the weather was good and there was peace on the line I brought his crib outside. Estella played with the little ones, and Luís...

Camera swish pans to a clump of juniper on the hillside in deep b.g. We can make out Luís, crouching there with several cronies, apparently plotting something.

Esperanza's voice: ...Luís was in school.

Camera swish pans to another part of the hill, closer to the picket post. Ramón can be seen reclining on the slope with several cronies. The men appear moody and depressed.

Esperanza's voice: Ramón came every day and sat on the hillside, just watching. The ladies—well, they criticized Ramón for not keeping the kids.

63

Back to picket post. Full shot. In b.g. women are crocheting, chatting as they march. The baby's crib, sheathed in mosquito netting, lies on a table outside coffee shack in f.g. Esperanza is changing the baby's diaper. Mrs. Salazar and Teresa are talking to her.

Wipe to: another angle. Trucks and Sheriff's cars can be seen parked near the picket line. The scabs and deputies stand in the trucks, jeering at the marching women.

> **Esperanza's voice:** For a while the Sheriff's men left us alone. But then it started again. They cursed us, insulted us, called us foul names. It started again.

Wipe to: the picket post. Wider angle, as a moving truck loaded with scabs tries to force its way through the living wall of women. The women try to push the truck back. They cling to it, and the scabs lean down and beat them off. The truck lurches forward, striking a woman and flinging her onto the road.

Several other women have opened the hood of the truck. They rip out ignition wires. The truck stalls.

Wipe to: the picket post. Long shot. The truck is gone. Four deputies wearing gas masks are firing tear gas shells into the picket line. The women retreat, fan out in a great arc.

> **Esperanza's voice:** They used tear gas again. This time the wind was against us.

Another angle, shooting toward hillslope. Esperanza and Estella can be seen running up the slope away from the gas. Esperanza carries the baby.

> **Esperanza's voice:** When that happened we spread out, as we had planned, and I took the baby away from the danger, as we had planned.

Back to picket post. Medium long shot. Instead of tear gas enveloping the picket line, the picket line envelops the drifting gas, re-forms again down-wind.

> **Esperanza's voice:** But they couldn't break our line. They couldn't break it . . .

Full shot: the road, below picket post, where a small army of scabs and deputies is gathered. The scabs stand sheepishly beside the trucks. The Sheriff, Barton, and several deputies are gazing off at the picket line. They are no longer amused. The superintendent's Cadillac enters scene, coming up the road. It rolls to a stop near the Sheriff's party.

Close group shot: at car.

> **Alexander** *(to Sheriff)*: Well?
> **Sheriff** *(hopelessly)*: I've tried everything but shootin' em down.
> **Alexander:** You haven't tried locking them up!
> **Sheriff** *(doubtfully)*: You want 'em *all* arrested?
> **Alexander:** No, just the ring leaders. The fire-eaters. And the ones with big families... *(to Barton)* Barton—where's that boy?
> **Barton** *(waves, shouts)*: Hey, you—c'mere.

Sebastian Prieto, the fingerman, leaves a group of deputies in b.g. and comes over. The Sheriff glances at him with contempt, then starts toward the picket line, Prieto and the deputies moving with him.

The picket line. Full shot, as they approach the line. The women keep on marching. Esperanza is among them, carrying the baby.

> **Sheriff** (shouting at them): Awright, girls—I'm gonna give you a choice—you can go home or you can go to jail. No ifs, ands or buts. Git off the picket line or git arrested.

Silence. The women keep on marching. The Sheriff turns to Sebastian.

> **Sheriff:** Okay. Point 'em out.
> **Sebastian** (a furtive mumble): That one—Teresa Vidal. She's the leader.

Kimbrough walks over to the line, grabs Teresa's arm as she marches by.

Closer angle, featuring Kimbrough and Teresa.

> **Kimbrough:** You're under arrest. Home or the hoosegow—what's it gonna be?

Several of the women stop marching. Mrs. Kalinsky picks up a stick. They approach Kimbrough menacingly.

> **Teresa:** Keep marching, sisters. Let's show some discipline.
> **Mrs. Kalinsky:** But Teresa, we...
> **Teresa:** They'll charge us with resisting arrest. Keep marching!

She jerks loose from Kimbrough and walks alone toward the trucks.

Back to Sheriff's group. Medium shot. As Sebastian fingers other women the deputies walk off one by one to arrest them.

> **Sebastian:** And Mrs. Salazar...the old one. And Chana Díaz— that one, in the blue dress. And Luz Morales, the little one, shaking her fist...and Mrs. Kalinsky, the Anglo...and Ruth Barnes, she's the organizer's wife...

The picket line. Medium shot, as the women are plucked off the line, one by one. They do not resist. We can see Esperanza still marching. She seems to clutch the baby more tightly to her. Estella tags along beside her mother.

Reverse angle, shooting toward trucks. The back of one truck is already filled with women, and the other is filling rapidly.

Two shot: Sheriff and Sebastian.

> **Sebastian:** . . . And Lala Alvarez, the pretty one over there. And that one.
> **Sheriff** *(irritably)*: With the baby?
> **Sebastian** *(a sly grin)*: She's Ramón Quintero's wife. He don't like her being here at all.

The Sheriff hesitates a moment, his eyes narrowed in thought, then gives Vance the nod. Vance approaches the line.

Medium shot: at picket line. Vance plucks at Esperanza's sleeve. She stops for a second, frightened, wavering. The women remaining on the line call out to her:

> **Ad libs** *(in Spanish)*:
> We'll take the baby, Esperanza . . .
> Don't worry about Juanito . . .
> We'll keep Estella too . . .

Vance pulls at her arm again. Esperanza stiffens with a sudden fierceness.

> **Esperanza:** No. The baby stays with me. *(She stoops down to Estella.)* Go to Papa. You stay with Papa, hear?

Head high, carrying the baby, Esperanza walks off toward the waiting trucks. The little girl watches her go, bereft, perplexed.

Ext., hillside. Close shot: Ramón. He comes to his feet, tense with anxiety.

Ext., picket line. Long panning shot from his angle. Suddenly Estella breaks away from the picket line and runs after her mother. Esperanza is climbing into the back of the second truck, which is now full. Estella jumps onto the tailgate and a woman pulls her up. We hear motors starting. The trucks pull off slowly. At the same instant we hear Teresa's clear voice, singing "Solidarity Forever." The other women join her. The chorus swells. Camera holds on the receding trucks, and the singing fades. Now Camera pans slowly back to the picket line. There are only a handful of women remaining. But from somewhere we hear the song again. Camera pans on, holds on a view of the wooded hillside. Suddenly we see twenty or more women coming down the slope with Consuelo

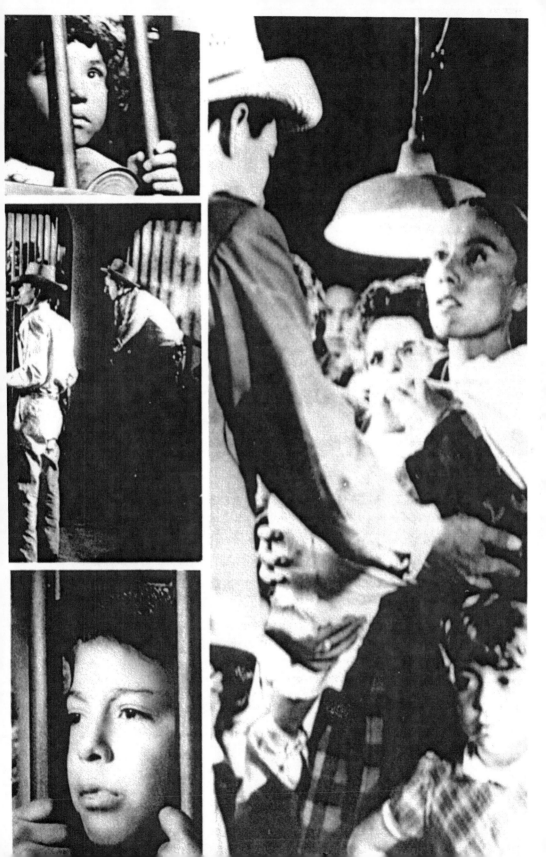

Ruíz in the lead. They are singing, these reserves, coming to replenish the gaps in the line.

Slow dissolve to: int., county jail: two cells. Full shot, night. Over the dissolve we hear the rhythmic clank of tin cups against steel bars. Lights come up slowly to reveal two adjacent jail cells packed with women. All are standing, for there is no room to sit down. The women in f.g. bang on the bars, and all of them chant rhythmically in Spanish:

Women:
Queremos comida...
Queremos camas...
Queremos baños...
Queremos comida...

Reverse two shot: Turnkey and Vance as seen from the cell. The two deputies are leaning back in their chairs against a blank wall opposite the cells. The deafening chant is driving the turnkey to distraction. He puts his hands to his ears. Suddenly he rises and comes over, holding up his hands for quiet. Vance follows.

> **Turnkey:** Now listen! Please, girls! Be quiet! Listen! *(The din subsides.)* I've told you ten times. We don't have no food. We don't have no beds. We don't have no baths. So please—*please—shut up!*

Vance grins at Luz Morales, whose face can be seen behind the bars in close foreground. He reaches out, chucks her under the chin. Luz scratches at his hand, and he withdraws it. The chant is resumed.

Int., rear of cell. Close group shot. The one cot in the cell is occupied by Estella and the infant Juanito. Juanito is crying. Esperanza hovers worriedly over him, trying to get him to take a nippled bottle, which he rejects.

> **Esperanza** *(to Teresa):* He can't drink this milk. It'll make him sick. He's on a formula. *(In a panic of guilt.)* I was a fool! I shouldn't have kept him with me.
> **Teresa:** Don't you worry. We'll get some action.

She moves off to the front of the cell, calling for quiet.

Front of cell, featuring Teresa. The women stop their clamor for a moment. Teresa calls out to Vance:

Teresa: The baby can't drink this store milk. We want his formula!
Vance (*puzzled*): You want what?
Ruth: The formula, the formula...

The women begin banging away with their cups again taking up the chant.

Women: We want the formula! We want the formula!

Vance winces at the noise.

Int., court house hallway. Medium shot, night. Ramón can be seen coming slowly up the hall. Luís trails behind him. Ramón walks like a man in enemy territory. From off scene the sound of the women's chant carries over: "We want the formula..."

The hall. Another angle. Ramón is passing a door marked: OFFICE OF THE DISTRICT ATTORNEY. The door is slightly ajar. Ramón stops, turns back, looks inside.

Int., District Attorney's office from Ramón's angle. All that can be seen in Ramón's cone of vision is a desk across the room. The D.A.'s feet are on the desk. He is in his shirt sleeves, but wearing his hat. Alexander sits on the corner of the desk. Hartwell and the sheriff wander in and out of scene, pacing the floor.

D.A.: Well, you can get the J.P. to swear out peace bonds. Or heist the bail high enough so you can keep 'em in jail.
Sheriff (*exasperated*): Keep 'em? What am I supposed to do—feed 'em outa my own pocket?

Back to hallway. Ramón and Luís. Ramón's hand is half-raised to the door-knob. It falls to his side. He listens.

D.A.'s voice: What I want to know, Mr. Hartwell, is when you gonna settle this thing. You won't negotiate with 'em. What are you after, anyway?

Medium shot: Hartwell from Ramón's angle.

Hartwell (*pacing*): The company has other mines. You've got to see the larger picture. Once these people get out of hand...

Without noticing Ramón, but conscious of the need to keep what he is saying confidential, Hartwell has moved to the door and closed it, cutting off the rest of his sentence.

Back to Ramón, frustrated in his desire to hear more. Just then Vance rounds a corner in b.g. and enters scene, walking toward Camera. He stops short, seeing Ramón. For a moment they stare at each other. Vance looks scared, despite the fact that he is armed and within his own bastille.

> **Vance:** What you doin' here? Ain't you seen enough of me?
> **Ramón** *(scarcely audible)*: I come for my kids. They're in your jail.

Vance warily brushes past Ramón and opens the office door, gesturing for the Sheriff. During the few moments the door is open we hear:

> **D.A.'s voice:** But you've played every trump in your hand and they're not dead yet.
> **Hartwell's voice:** Not every trump.
> **D.A.'s voice:** Such as what?

The Sheriff comes out, closing the door behind him, cutting off the inside conversation again.

> **Vance:** I can't shut them dames up. They keep yellin' about the formula.
> **Sheriff:** The what?
> **Vance:** Formula for the baby or somethin'. *(Indicates Ramón.)* His kid.

The Sheriff glances at Ramón and stalks off down the hall. Vance follows.

Int., jail corridor, shooting toward cells, as the Sheriff and Vance enter. The women's clamor is as loud as ever. The Sheriff holds up his hands for quiet.

> **Sheriff:** Now look here. I got you some milk for the baby. So what's all the belly-achin' about?
> **Ad lib:** It's no good, the milk . . .
> Queremos la formula . . .
> The baby has a formula . . .
> If Juanito gets sick you'll be responsible . . .
> **Sheriff** *(exasperated)*: I'm not running a drug store. You girls got nobody but yourselves to blame and you can be home with your families in an hour. All you have to do is sign a pledge that you won't go back to the picket line.

Many voices *(in English and Spanish)*:
Don't sign nothin' for the stinker.
No, no deals, no deals...
Make him get the formula.

They start banging on the bars again. The sheriff turns angrily to Vance.

Sheriff: Where'd that fellow go?

Vance takes a few steps, shouts around a corner, beckoning.

Vance: Hey, Pancho, c'mere!

Ramón enters scene, walking slowly into f.g. Luís tags along behind. The women fall silent abruptly. It is very still.

Close group shot: at cell door. The Sheriff motions to the turnkey to unlock one of the cells. He obeys.

Sheriff: Awright. Where's the baby? And the little girl?

Esperanza brings the baby from the rear of the cell. Estella squeezes past the tightly packed women, joins her mother. Ramón and Esperanza gaze at each other with deep poignancy, unsmiling. He holds out his hands. She gives the baby to him. Estella looks up at her mother. Esperanza nods, gives her a little push. Estella walks outside. Luís takes her hand. The father and his children walk off slowly, out of scene. The women watch them go. The turnkey locks the cell again. Suddenly they start banging on the bars.

Voices:
Queremos comida...
Queremos camas...
Queremos baños...
Queremos comida...

Dissolve to: ext., Quintero back yard. Full shot, day. The shot matches the earlier scene of Luz and Esperanza—but now Ramón and Antonio are hanging out the wash. Estella and the little Morales boy are there. Ramón sees them playing in the baskets.

Ramón: Will you kids get out of those baskets!

There are two large wicker baskets beside the fence: one contains Juani-

to, the other a mountain of damp clothes. As he works, Antonio calls from across the fence:

> **Antonio** *(in Spanish):* How goes it?
> **Ramón:** *(in Spanish):* It never ends.

He snaps out a damp undershirt, hangs it up. Suddenly he explodes:

> **Ramón:** Three hours! Just to heat enough water to wash this stuff! *(A pause. He goes on working.)* I tell you something. If this strike is ever settled—which I doubt—I don't go back to work unless the company installs hot running water for us. *(Another pause.)* It should've been a union demand from the beginning.
> **Antonio:** Yeah.

We hear the baby wail. Ramón walks over to the basket, puts the nipple of the bottle back in Juanito's mouth. Then he resumes his chores. Antonio muses as he works.

> **Antonio:** It's like Charley Vidal says—there's two kinds of slavery, wage slavery and domestic slavery. The Woman Question, he calls it.
> **Ramón:** The woman...*question?*
> **Antonio:** Question, question—the problem, what to do about 'em.
> **Ramón** *(cautious):* So? What does he want to do about 'em?

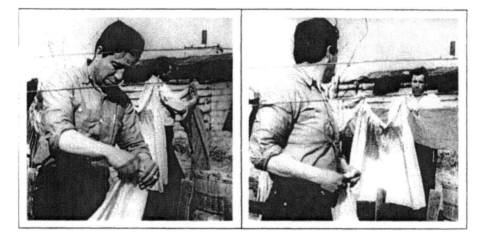

Antonio: He says give 'em equality. Equality in jobs, equality in the home. Also sex equality.

Ramón *(a long pause):* What do you mean—sex equality?

Antonio: You know... *(Leers, shifts into Spanish.)* What's good for the goose is good for the gander.

Close shot: Ramón with a clothespin in his mouth, mulling over this concept. His imagination runs away with him. He scowls thoughtfully.

Antonio's voice: He's some organizer, that Charley. He can organize a wife right out of your home.

Ramón bites viciously on a clothespin and hangs up a pair of diapers.

Dissolve to: int., Quintero kitchen. Medium shot, night. There are two large tubs on the cluttered drainboard—one of soapy water, one of rinse water. Ramón is washing the dishes. Luís is drying them. Ramón is sweaty and sullen. Luís is bored and impatient.

Luís: Papa, can't I leave now? There's a meeting of the Junior Shop Stewards...

Ramón: The what!

Luís: The Junior Shop Stewards. There's lots of ways we can help.

Ramón *(exploding):* Don't I have enough troubles without them shipping you off to reform school?

Luís *(earnestly)*: But, Papa—you need all the help you can get.

Ramón: You've got to help around the house!

Luís: But you've got me doing everything. Mama never used to make me dry the...

Ramón *(cutting him off)*: You should have helped her without being asked.

At that moment we hear the raucous braying of an automobile horn from outside. Luís dashes into the parlor. Ramón stands there scrubbing a greasy dish. Now we hear gay laughter, and then, in Spanish:

Charley's voice: ¡Buenas noches!

Esperanza's voice: Hasta mañana, Charley.

Int., parlor. Full shot: shooting toward front door. Ramón enters scene f.g., stops. The front door bursts open, Esperanza enters. She embraces Luís. He grins, responding with a shy, awkward hug. Esperanza looks at Ramón. Her face is aglow. She looks younger and heartier than we have ever seen her. She comes quickly into close foreground, embracing Ramón. He puts his arms around her—but stiffly, withholding himself. She looks up at him lovingly.

Ramón: How do you feel?

Esperanza: I'm okay. But it's nice to be home.

Ramón: Four nights. How did you sleep?

Esperanza: We raised such a fuss they finally brought cots in. *(She laughs; her hand goes to her throat.)* I nearly lost my voice, yelling so much. *(suddenly)* How's Estellita? And the baby? *(She goes out.)*

Ramón *(following her)*: They're asleep.

Int., bedroom. Medium shot. The bedroom is dark. Esperanza and Ramón are only moving shadows. Dimly we see her hovering over the crib. Ramón whispers.

Ramón: Did you have to sign a pledge? Not to go back to the line?

Esperanza *(a whisper)*: No, no...we wouldn't do it.

From off scene we hear a knock at the front door. Esperanza crosses the dark room to answer it, Ramón following.

Ramón *(a whisper)*: But if you go back they'll lock you up again.

Esperanza *(whispering):* No, no...the Sheriff had enough of us. We drove him crazy. *(She goes out.)*

Int., parlor. Full shot. Esperanza opens the front door, admitting three women: Teresa, Ruth and Consuelo. They enter beaming, excited.

> **Teresa:** It's all set. Consuelo's squad can take the day off tomorrow. We're taking over.
> **Esperanza** *(ushering them in):* Good. Come in, we'll work it out. Sit down, sit down.

The three women sit down on the couch. Esperanza crosses to the dining table to get a chair for herself. Ramón is standing there.

Two shot: Ramón and Esperanza. He is the stern patriarch now. As she reaches for the chair he says, sotto voce:

> **Ramón:** We've got to have a talk, you and me.
> **Esperanza:** All right, but later. I've got a meeting now.
> **Ramón** *(suppressed outrage):* A meeting?
> **Esperanza:** Yes. To plan for the picket line tomorrow.

She walks off with her chair. Camera holds on Ramón. He is burning. We hear:

> **Esperanza's voice:** Now—let's see...who's available?
> **Teresa's voice:** Chana's husband is out of town—on that delegation to see the governor. And Anita Gonzales' husband, too...
> **Consuelo's voice:** And six or seven others—Lala's husband and Mariana's...

Ramón looks like he's about to explode.

Int., parlor. Full shot. As Ramón strides toward the front door, we hear:

> **Ruth:** And there's a whole bunch of men going on a fuel-hunting expedition—thirty or forty of them—so their wives are out too.
> **Esperanza:** But we can ask them to keep our kids, so the rest of us can...

Ramón exits, slamming the door loudly behind him. The women react with a what's-eating-him look. Teresa turns sympathetically to Esperanza.

> **Teresa:** What are you going to do about him, Esperanza?

Consuelo: It's time he was house broken. Maybe if a delegation of us talked to him . . .

Esperanza *(deeply upset):* No, no . . . I have to work it out with him myself.

Dissolve to: int., beer parlor. Full shot: the bar, night. Seven miners are seated on stools at the bar, drinking beer. These are the disconsolate ones—the defeated and perplexed, the traditionalist hold-outs and the unwilling babysitters. An atmosphere of gloom pervades the place. Their backs are to Camera, but seated from left to right they are: Jenkins, Antonio, two unidentified miners (whom we have seen around the picket line), Cente Cavazos, José Sanchez and Ramón. The bartender, an Anglo, is a beefy, easy-going fellow with a friendly manner. He sets fresh beers before a couple of miners, but no money changes hands. We see the bartender mark something on a tab at the register. Camera moves on to the next miner, an Anglo, leaning moodily on his elbow.

Anglo miner: I got a friend, he's got a friend in the Bureau of Mines. Know what he says? They ain't never gonna open up that mine again.

Fourth miner: How come?

Anglo miner *(as Camera moves past him):* He says the ore's played out. So help me.

Cente: Could be.

Camera holds on Ramón. There's a whiskey glass and a bottle of beer before him. Ramón is in a sodden blue funk.

Ramón: Bull. Lotta bull. That's a rich mine. I know.

He drinks off his whiskey, chases it down with beer, then stares moodily at the empty glass.

Ramón: But what's the difference? They'll never settle with us. Never.

Suddenly we hear an excited shout:

Antonio's voice: Hey! Hey! What d'ya know!

Full shot: miners at bar. Antonio holds up a magazine, stabbing a picture with his finger.

78

Antonio: It's him! It's him! El Presidente! The President of the Company.

All the miners except Ramón get off their stools and come over, looking at the picture.

Antonio: Listen to this: *(reading)* "MAN OF DISTINCTION. J. Hamilton Miller, financier, business executive, Board Chairman of Continental Factors, and president of Delaware Zinc Incorporated. An enthusiastic sportsman and expert marksman, Mr. Miller manages to find time every year for an African safari. He leaves this month for Kenya, where he hopes to bag his thirteenth lion!"

There is a long silence. The men stare at the portrait—with hatred, with despair. Antonio rips the page out of the magazine.

Antonio: I'm gonna frame this. *(turning)* Hey, Ramón—look.

Ramón just grunts with disgust. He sips his beer.

Ramón *(absently):* Got to look at the larger picture.

A pall falls over the group again. The miners return to their bar stools.

Close moving shot (as before).

Jenkins *(staring into space):* How do you like that? The guy is a lion hunter.
Antonio: What d'you expect him to hunt—rabbits?
Fourth miner: Man, oh man. I'd sure like to get me some venison.
Cente: I ain't tasted meat in four weeks. *(suddenly)* How about it, Ramón? Let's take off for a couple of days, huh?
Ramón *(after a long pause):* Why ask me? Am I runnin' this strike? If you want permission to go over the hill, go ask the Ladies Auxiliary.

He drains his beer, rises and stalks off.

Dissolve to: full shot, night: int. Quintero bedroom, dimly lit by one small lamp. Esperanza appears to be asleep. Ramón enters, crosses to the bed and sits down heavily. He begins to remove his shoes. Camera moves in. Esperanza's eyes come open, in the way of one who has been wide awake. Without moving she says in quiet reproach:

Esperanza: I waited up till midnight.

Ramón (*not looking at her*): You weren't waiting for *me*.

Esperanza: That meeting only lasted ten minutes. (*A pause. Then quietly.*) The first night I'm home, and you run to the beer parlor. What is it? Can't you bear the sight of me?

Ramón (*fierce whisper*): Be still...

Esperanza: But you wanted to talk. Tell me.

He rises suddenly and goes out. Esperanza slips out of bed, flings on a dressing gown.

Int., kitchen. Medium shot, night. Ramón has a cup and is pouring coffee from the pot on the stove. Esperanza enters scene, stands in the doorway.

Esperanza: Tell me.

Ramón (*not looking at her*): We can't go on this way. I just can't ...go on living with you. Not this way.

Esperanza (*softly*): No. We can't go on this way. We can't go back to the old way either.

Ramón sips his coffee, glares at her.

Ramón: The *old way?* What's your "new way"? What's it mean? Your "right" to neglect your kids?

He goes abruptly to the parlor. Esperanza stands there a moment, then slowly follows him.

Int., parlor. Full shot. Ramón goes to a closet, gets a rifle and a box of shells off the shelf. He sits down on the edge of a chair and begins to clean the rifle with an oily rag. Esperanza enters scene, watching him. There is a long silence.

Esperanza: Where are you going?

Ramón: Hunting.

Esperanza: When?

Ramón: Sun up.

Esperanza: Alone?

Ramón: No.

Esperanza (*after a pause*): Ramón—you can't.

Ramón: Why not? I'm not needed here.

Esperanza: But you *are* needed. Especially now—with most of the other men away. You're captain of the stand-by squad.

Ramón *(bitterly)*: Sure, the stand-by squad. Stand-by for the funeral.

Esperanza: Whose funeral? We're doing all right. There hasn't been a scab near the picket line for three days.

Ramón: And you know why? Because the company knows they can starve us out—even if it takes another two, three months. What's it to them if the mine's shut down a little longer?

Esperanza: It's a lot to them. They'd do anything to open that mine.

Ramón: Aah! They've got other mines. You don't see the larger picture. *(A pause.)* They've got millions. Millions. They can out-last us, and they know it.

Esperanza: You mean you're ready to give up?

Ramón *(flaring)*: Who said anything about giving up? I'll never go back to the company on my knees. Never.

He pulls back the bolt of the rifle, inserts a cartridge, tests the bolt.

Esperanza: You want to go down fighting, is that it? *(He shrugs.)* I don't want to go down fighting. I want to win.

No response. She walks over to him, Camera following.

Esperanza: Ramón...we're not getting weaker. We're stronger than ever before. *(He snorts with disgust.)* They're getting weaker. They thought they could break our picket line. And they failed. And now they can't win unless they pull off something big, and pull it off fast.

Ramón: Like what?

Esperanza: I don't know. But I can feel it coming. It's like...like a lull before the storm. Charley Vidal says...

Ramón *(exploding)*: Charley Vidal says! *(He rises, flinging rifle aside.)* Don't throw Charley Vidal up to me!

Esperanza: Charley's my friend. I need friends. *(She looks at him strangely.)* Why are you afraid to have me as your friend?

Ramón: I don't know what you're talking about.

Esperanza: No, you don't. Have you learned nothing from this strike? Why are you afraid to have me at your side? Do you still think you can have dignity only if I have none?

Ramón: You talk of dignity? After what you've been doing?

Esperanza: Yes. I talk of dignity. The Anglo bosses look down on you, and you hate them for it. "Stay in your place, you dirty Mexican"—that's what they tell you. But why must you say to me, "Stay in *your* place"? Do you feel better having someone lower than you?

Ramón: Shut up, you're talking crazy.

But Esperanza moves right up to him, speaking now with great passion.

Esperanza: Whose neck shall I stand on, to make me feel superior? And what will I get out of it? I don't want anything lower than I am. I'm low enough already. I want to rise. And push everything up with me as I go . . .

Ramón *(fiercely):* Will you be still?

Esperanza *(shouting):* And if you can't understand this you're a fool—because you can't win this strike without me! You can't win *anything* without me!

He seizes her shoulder with one hand, half raises the other to slap her. Esperanza's body goes rigid. She stares straight at him, defiant and unflinching. Ramón drops his hand.

Esperanza: That would be the old way. Never try it on me again—never.

She crosses to the doorway, then turns back.

Esperanza: I am going to bed now. Sleep where you please—but not with me.

She goes out. Fade out.

Fade in: ext., picket post. Full shot, early morning. Dispirited and shivering, the women march, hunched against the wind. Near the coffee shack is an oil drum in which a wood fire is burning. Teresa, the picket captain, walks toward Esperanza. Teresa closely watches Esperanza's dejected face.

Two shot: at oil drum. The two women warm their hands over the fire. Teresa muses:

Teresa: So they had a little taste of what it's like to be a woman . . . . and they run away.

Esperanza: With Ramón it's... pride. I spoke out of the bitterness in me. And he was hurt.

Esperanza stares at the fire. Teresa looks at her with deep sympathy.

Teresa: Anything worth learning is a hurt. These changes come with pain... for other husbands too... not just Ramón.

Dissolve to: ext., mountain landscape. Long panning shot, day. A vista of wild and lonely beauty. A cold wind rustles the junipers and pine of a steep boulder-strewn arroyo. The deer hunters can be seen walking up a narrow trail in single file. They are bunched together, save for Ramón, who lags behind.

Medium panning shot, featuring Ramón. He walks slowly up the trail into f.g., brooding. As he walks he hears Esperanza's voice of the preceding night, hauntingly.

Esperanza's voice: You mean you're ready to give up? *(Pause.)* I don't want to go down fighting. I want to win. *(Pause.)* Have you learned nothing from this strike? *(Pause.)* I can feel it coming. It's like a lull before the storm. *(Pause.)* And now they can't win unless they pull off something big and pull it off fast.

A shot is heard ringing through the arroyo. It pulls Ramón up short. He calls to the other men, suddenly:

Ramón: Brothers, we've got to go back!

Ext., picket post: wide angle at drum, including truck. Charley is at the wheel, Sal beside him. The truck stops near the oil drum. Charley leans out, calls urgently.

Charley: Esperanza! Where's Ramón?
Esperanza *(dully)*: Ramón?
Sal: Did he go hunting with the others?
Charley *(as Esperanza nods)*: Where? Where can we find him? Do you know?
Esperanza: No.

During this exchange several women have left the picket line and come over.

Sal *(muttering bitterly):* Deer hunters! Deserters, that's what they are.

Teresa: Something wrong? *(insistently)* Charley, tell us.

Charley *(reluctantly):* Company's got an eviction order.

Dissolve to: series of shots: large close shot of young woman crying "EVICTION!" "EVICTION!" Large close shot young boy crying "EVICTION! EVICTION! EVICTION!" Woman at clothesline hearing the call and leaving. Woman at kitchen door calling out "Where?" and leaving. Truck on road stops. Man runs in, calls, "EVICTION! At the Quintero place." Car on road is stopped by several women; they pile in, the car pulls away. Shots of people walking, by twos and by groups, finally passing the car in which are seated Alexander and Hartwell.

Alexander *(to a perturbed Hartwell):* Don't worry. Quintero's gone hunting with the others. Evict him first; the rest will be easy. Let their neighbors watch. Scare some sense into them.

Dissolve to: ext., road and company housing. Long shot. The sheriff's convoy is drawn up outside a row of company houses. We can see deputies milling about in the front yard of one of the cottages, and a cluster of women watching them from outside the fence.

Ext., cottage: closer angle. It is the Quintero place. The Sheriff stands in the front yard, directing operations. His deputies are lugging furniture out of the house. They dump it in the yard or at the side of the road. Several of them emerge from the front door with the Quinteros' bed. Esperanza, Luz and a dozen other women silently watch the eviction from outside the fence. Mrs. Salazar is there with a bevy of kids (including Juanito whom she holds in her arms). The only man present is the parish priest.

Ext., main road, Zinc Town. Long panning shot. We pick up Jenkins' car loaded with the stand-by squad roaring toward the housing area. The car passes the store, the church, the school. As the car comes into f.g., and moves on out of scene, Camera holds on the school playground. In the distance we see Luís beckoning to a number of his companions. The boys set off at a run up the road.

Back to company housing. Group shot: women, featuring Esperanza and Luz.

Luz: Can't we do something?

No answer from Esperanza. She moves toward the front gate. Other women follow her. Camera pans with them. Just then the deputy Kimbrough comes through the gate carrying a lamp and a vase. He dumps them onto the road. The vase breaks. He shoves Esperanza roughly away from the gate.

Kimbrough: All right, girls—get back, get back.

Reverse angle: shooting past convoy, as Jenkins' car swerves around the tail of the convoy, comes on up the road, stops near the cottage. Ramón and the others pile out. They join the throng of women. Ramón carries his rifle purposefully.

Group shot: women and priest watching the deputies as Ramón comes to Esperanza's side. She sees him. Her face lights up. Ramón's eyes meet hers for a moment. He is unsmiling. Then he looks away at:

The deputies, from his angle, dumping the precious accumulations of a lifetime onto the road: the shrine, a kewpie doll, a faded photograph.

Close shot: portrait of Juárez. It falls in the dust. The frame breaks.

Back to watchers, featuring Ramón, his face working in hatred and anger. Esperanza is beside him now. He brings the barrel of his rifle up as if to level it. She glances at him in terror. Suddenly Ramón goes slack; the shadow of defeat crosses his face. With an abrupt movement he thrusts the rifle on Mrs. Salazar—who takes it, blinking with surprise.

Ext., cottage. Full shot from their angle. Four deputies are emerging from the front door burdened with the ancient iron stove. Camera pans away from them, holds on the fence separating the Quintero and Morales yards. Now we see Luís and his cronies pop up from behind the fence. Each boy holds a grass-tailed clod. They let fly. Camera swish pans back to the porch—and we see two of the clods hit their target, spattering the deputies with dirt. One deputy drops his corner of the stove, and it crashes down the steps. Several other deputies take off after the boys, leaving the gate unguarded. The sheriff yells:

Sheriff: Never mind them brats! Come on—get the work done.

Reverse angle, featuring tenants. Other women, children and old men are arriving on the scene. There are now over twenty women watching the eviction but there is no excitement, no talk.

Closer angle, featuring Ramón and Esperanza. Ramón is calmer now, but alert, planning, thinking. He looks around at their gathering forces— not yet impressive, but growing every moment. He almost smiles with slow realization.

> **Ramón** *(half to himself):* This is what we've been waiting for.
> **Esperanza** *(anxious, puzzled):* What are you saying?
> **Ramón:** This means they've given up trying to break the picket line. *(A pause.)* Now we can *all* fight together—all of us.

Suddenly he draws Esperanza close, whispers something in her ear. She nods, turns swiftly to several other women, huddles with them a moment.

Camera pans with the women as they enter the yard, swooping down to pick up household belongings on their way.

Ext., front yard. Full shot. Other women, seeing what Esperanza and her sisters are up to, swiftly join them in the yard, begin to pick up furniture and carry it back into the house by way of the rear door. Deputies emerging from the house, loaded down with furniture and bric-a-brac, find themselves passing women loaded with objects they have just deposited

in the yard. One of the deputies stops in close f.g., staring at the women in slack-jawed bafflement. Ramón glances at Mrs. Salazar. He winks. Mrs. Salazar smiles. It is the first time we have seen her smile.

Back to yard, featuring **Sheriff**. His deputies are hopelessly dispersed. Half of them are chasing the boys, while the furniture-moving contingent is out-numbered by women crowding into the yard. The Sheriff wheels right and left in helpless exasperation. He spots Ramón near the front fence, strides over to him.

> **Sheriff** (bellowing): Now see here, Quintero! These women are obstructin' justice. You make 'em behave, savvy?
> **Ramón:** I can't do nothing, Sheriff. You know how it is—they won't listen to a man any more.
> **Sheriff** (blustering): You want me to lock 'em up again?
> **Ramón** (smiles): You want 'em in your lock-up again?

The Sheriff stalks off, fuming.

Ext., road and yard. Full shot. More women keep arriving all the time.

Several small fry, imitating their mothers, run into the yard, pick up lamps, pots, pans, etc., and return them to the house.

A side road. Medium long shot. Two cars pull up and stop near the convoy. Consuelo Ruíz and six other women get out, approach the cottage.

The yard. Full shot. From off scene we hear the blast of an automobile horn, while from the middle of the yard the Sheriff bellows at his men:

> **Sheriff:** Form a cordon! Keep 'em away from the house! Form a cordon!

Ext., road. Medium long shot: past convoy. Two other cars pull up at the tail of the convoy. Frank Barnes and a half-dozen miners get out, hurry toward the Quintero cottage.

Back to yard. Full shot. By now the Sheriff's men have reassembled and are forming a cordon, from the porch steps to the front gate, permitting no one else to enter the yard. Four deputies pick up the Quinteros' bed and begin to carry it toward the truck. When they reach the gate they find it blocked by the six new miners and four of Ramón's stand-by squad. The deputies stop, ease their burden to the ground. Just then we hear a klaxon from o.s. Everyone turns to see:

Another convoy. Long panning shot. The union truck is in the lead. Charley Vidal is at the wheel, and the back of the truck is loaded with a dozen miners. Following it are a half-dozen miners' cars. The union convoy rolls past the parked Sheriff's convoy, draws to a stop in f.g. The miners tumble out, move in a body toward the gate of the Quintero cottage. They are all big men, and their faces are grim and determined. We count fifteen, twenty, twenty-five, thirty of them.

Close group shot: miners at gate looking at their approaching brothers. Alfredo nudges Gonzales.

> **Alfredo:** Hey! The guys from the open pit...
> **Gonzales:** And the guys from the mill.

Ext., cottage and yard. Full shot (boom shot if possible). Ramón, Esperanza and other women and children re-emerge from the house, stop on the porch in a compact mass. Facing them outside the gate are forty miners. The deputies are in between. They stir nervously, glancing from side to side. No one says anything. A heavy stillness falls over the yard.

Now we see other women and children closing in at the side fence: then Luís and a half-dozen other boys appear at the opposite fence. The Sheriff is in dead center of this shot. Without realizing it, he makes a full turn of 360°, looking at his adversaries.

His angle. Slow panning shot. The Sheriff's forces are completely surrounded by over a hundred men, women and children. Appearing on the surrounding hills, on every side, are other miners, other women, other kids—massed, impassive.

Full shot: the Sheriff turning, staring at the massed power against him. With an abrupt, frustrated gesture the Sheriff waves to his men to follow and walks out the gate. The miners break ranks to let him pass. When the last deputy has left the yard the men close ranks and face the convoy. Still there is no voice, no sound save the starting motors.

The road and yard. Full shot, as seen from the porch. Shooting past the miners outside the gate. The convoy lurches into motion. The men watch it till the last car has passed. Then they turn to face the women, who enter scene f.g., moving down the steps, meeting the men in the yard. Suddenly someone laughs and then there is a release in laughter running through the crowd, and we hear half-whispered, awed comment.

> **Ad libs** (*English and Spanish*):
> We stopped them . . .
> It took all we had, but we stopped them . . .
> When we heard about it at the mill, we just walked off . . .
> Did you see their faces? . . .

The receding convoy. Long panning shot. The convoy approaches a crossroad a quarter of a mile downhill from the Quintero house. We see a Cadillac parked there at the corner. The lead car of the convoy stops and the Sheriff gets out. He walks over to the Cadillac.

Close shot: at Cadillac. Alexander and Hartwell are sitting there. The Sheriff starts to speak, then closes his mouth again. He indicates his empty trucks with a helpless gesture.

> **Sheriff:** Got any more ideas?
> **Alexander** (*defensively, passing the buck*): I don't make policy.

He looks at Hartwell. Hartwell puffs on a cigarette. After a long pause he says:

Hartwell: I'll talk to New York. Maybe we better settle this thing. *(Another puff)* For the present.

Back to Quintero yard. Full shot. Part of the milling throng has already dispersed; those who remain are carrying the last of the Quinteros' possessions back into the house. We see Luís jump the fence and run toward his mother in f.g. She gives him a fierce hug.

Medium shots at front gate. Ramón approaches Mrs. Salazar. He takes the baby from her arms. Estella enters the gate, dragging the portrait of Juárez. Solemnly she lifts up the portrait. Ramón takes it. He walks back toward the porch, Estella at his side.

The yard, shooting from the porch. Esperanza and Luís stand on the porch steps in f.g. Reaching them, Ramón turns, looks back at his friends, some of whom are still in the yard. They seem to be waiting for him to speak.

> **Esperanza's voice:** We did not know then that we had won the strike. But our hearts were full. And when Ramón said...
> **Ramón** *(simply):* Thanks... sisters... and brothers.

The people smile softly. A few of them lift their hands in a wave of acknowledgment. They begin to leave.

Close up shot: the Quintero family on porch. Ramón holds the baby in the crook of his arm. He hands the portrait of Juárez to Luís. The boy gazes at it with respect, wipes the dust off it, and readjusts the torn frame. Ramón heaves a long sigh. Unsmiling, he looks off at the receding convoy. Esperanza watches him. There is a pause. Still not looking at her, Ramón says haltingly:

> **Ramón:** Esperanza... thank you... for your dignity.

Esperanza's eyes fill with tears.

> **Ramón:** You were right. Together we can push everything up with us as we go.
> **Esperanza's voice:** Then I knew we had won something they could never take away—something I could leave to our children —and they, the salt of the earth, would inherit it.

Esperanza places her hand in Ramón's. With the children they walk into the house. Fade out.

90

FILM
CREDITS

Writer:
Michael Wilson

Director:
Herbert Biberman

Producer:
Paul Jarrico

Music:
Sol Kaplan

Associate Producers:
Sonja Dahl Biberman
Adolfo Barela

Assistant Directors:
Jules Schwerin
David Wolfe

Camera:
Leonard Stark
Stanley Meredith

Editors:
Ed Spiegel
Joan Laird

Sound:
Dick Stanton
Harry Smith

Stills:
Vernon Smith

Production Manager:
Jules Schwerin

Other Technicians:
Paul Perlin
Robert Ames
Irving Hentschel
Harry Reif

Herman Lipney
Fred Hudson
John Mathias
Marcia Endore
Mel Kells
Irving Fajans

PROFESSIONAL CAST

Esperanza Quintero:
Rosaura Revueltas

Sheriff:
Will Geer

Barton:
David Wolfe

Hartwell:
Mervin Williams

Alexander:
David Sarvis

NONPROFESSIONAL CAST

Ramón Quintero:
Juan Chacón

Teresa Vidal:
Henrietta Williams

Charley Vidal:
Ernest Velásquez

Consuelo Ruíz:
Angela Sánchez

Sal Ruíz:
Joe T. Morales

Luz Morales:
Clorinda Alderette

Antonio Morales:
Charles Coleman

Ruth Barnes:
Virginia Jencks

Frank Barnes:
Clinton Jencks

Vance:
E.A. Rockwell

Kimbrough:
William Rockwell

Luís Quintero:
Frank Talavera

Estella Quintero:
Mary Lou Castillo

Jenkins:
Floyd Bostick

Sebastian Prieto:
Victor Torres

Kalinsky:
E.S. Conerly

Mrs. Salazar:
Elvira Molano

Other Miners:
Adolfo Barela
Albert Muñoz

*And the Brothers
and Sisters of
Local 890,
International
Union of Mine, Mill,
and Smelter
Workers, Bayard,
New Mexico*

Presented by Independent Productions Corporation (Simon Lazarus, President) and the International Union of Mine, Mill, and Smelter Workers. Shot in New Mexico in 1953. Premiered in New York City in 1954.

SALT OF THE EARTH

Commentary by
Deborah Silverton Rosenfelt

PROLOGUE

> If trade unionists someday discover that this picture is the first
> feature film ever made in this country of labor, by labor, and for
> labor; if minority peoples come to see in it a film that does not tol-
> erate minorities but celebrates their greatness; if men and women
> together find in it some new recognition of the worth and dignity
> of a working-class woman—then this audience, these judges, will
> find ways of overcoming the harassment.—*Herbert Biberman and*
> *Paul Jarrico, "Breaking Ground," 1953*[1] *

I first saw *Salt of the Earth* in 1972 at a benefit for a new women's center
on the west side of Los Angeles. Like others in the audience, I was deeply moved. *Salt of the Earth* seemed to articulate the aspirations of women
of my generation: "I want to rise. And push everything up with me as I
go." Here was a film that presented housework, child care, sanitation as
important political issues; that used humor to deflate macho attitudes;
that recognized the necessity of rejecting the "old way" but acknowledged
the difficulty of creating something new; that had chosen a woman as
protagonist and entrusted to her the role of narrator. Here was that rarity,
a female hero who not only struggles and suffers but grows and wins.
And she gains not simply in self-knowledge, not simply through wresting
a piece of her own turf from an unchanged society; rather, her victory
represents the shared triumph of the community—the specific victory of a

*Notes appear on pages 154-168.

successful strike, the less tangible victory of greater equality between Anglos and Mexican-Americans, women and men.

The union organizer who showed the film that night[2] told us that *Salt of the Earth* was based on a real strike and that the women and men of the New Mexico mining community had played most of the major roles. The film, made in 1953, was the product of an unusual collaboration between Hollywood people blacklisted during the Truman-McCarthy era and the members of New Mexico Local 890 of the International Union of Mine, Mill, and Smelter Workers. I began to show it regularly to my classes; inevitably it was a high point of the semester. We wondered about it both as a work of art and as an interpretation of history: Where did its consciousness come from? What had happened in the real strike? How faithfully had it shaped life and art? How real and enduring was the victory at its conclusion? I began to learn more about its origins, to respect still more its role in the struggle for social change.

The outspoken feminism of *Salt of the Earth* is rare in films of any era, particularly rare in the fifties when the feminine mystique exerted so powerful a hold. Its portrayal of women's daily lives and its vision of growing power through growing sisterhood have made the film deeply welcome in the culture of the contemporary women's movement. Its story, though, must be one of struggle on many fronts. The effort to make the film came out of a complex struggle of ideologies that turned into ugly persecution during the heyday of Senator McCarthy. The effort to complete and distribute it was an uphill battle against a thoroughgoing boycott. In the strike that inspired it, long-standing conflicts between workers and owners, between Mexican-Americans and Anglos, merged with more recent tensions between women and men as the picket line altered their roles and their consciousness. The struggle of workers, of Mexican-Americans, of women for dignity and equality are the substance of *Salt of the Earth*. The film's significance today is its insistence on their relatedness, its vision of what director Herbert Biberman called "the indivisibility of equality"—and its acknowledgment of how hard it is to make that vision work.

The film encountered vicious opposition at every stage of production, post-production, and distribution. Herbert Biberman's book, *Salt of the Earth: The Story of a Film* (Boston: Beacon, 1965), gives an angry account of the obstacle course it had to run: congressional red-baiting, local vigilantism, a lockout from Hollywood's technical facilities, a boycott by most exhibitors.[3] In 1954, when the film was abortively released, even those American reviewers who liked it—among them Bosley Crowther of the New York *Times,* Roy Ringer of the Los Angeles *Daily News,* Luther Nichols of the San Francisco *Chronicle,* and the reviewer for *Time* Magazine—either qualified their praise by admitting that it was "slanted" or apologized for their admiration by emphasizing the Americanism of its values. Pauline Kael's review is especially symptomatic of the spirit of the age. The film, she wrote, was "as clear a piece of Communist propaganda as we have had in many years," nothing more nor less than "a proletarian morality play."[4] That Kael, a woman, could write a lengthy review virtually ignoring the feminist dimension of the film and labeling its story "ridiculously and patently false" measures the difference in consciousness between that era and our own.

Yet *Salt of the Earth* was well-received abroad when it first appeared. In 1954, it won the Grand Prize at Karlovy Vary, Czechoslovakia's international film festival. In 1956, it won the Académie du Cinéma de Paris award for the best film made anywhere in the world to be exhibited during the preceding year in France. It is still winning prizes overseas; on its recent release in Denmark, the Danish Association of Film Critics named it one of the ten best features of 1975. The film is popular in socialist countries; Russians, Cubans, and Chinese have seen it in regular theaters. It has been shown in tents in Algeria, veiled women standing quietly in the back. Portugal requested a print one week after the fall of the rightist regime in 1975.

In the United States, *Salt of the Earth* has been systematically denied regular commercial distribution. However, the sixteen-millimeter version—prints often pirated, often technically inferior—has been shown widely throughout the country, on college campuses, in union halls, at benefits and fund-raisers for a variety of causes. In 1975, Sonja Dahl Biberman, associate producer and scriptperson of *Salt of the Earth,* arranged a special screening of the film as part of the Laemmle Theaters' Emerging Women series. It was shown, as it should be, in a darkened theater in thirty-five millimeter. After the second showing at 1:00 A.M. that Sunday, screenwriter Michael Wilson rose to answer questions. The theater was packed; the audience gave him a standing ovation. The applause acknowledged the merit and significance of the film. And it welcomed both Wilson and *Salt of the Earth* back from the shadowy world of the blacklisted.

Young audiences today, seeing *Salt of the Earth* for the first time, often express surprise that so "old" a film should portray with such passionate comprehension the sometimes conflicting claims of feminist, ethnic, and class consciousness—issues still very much with us, conflicting claims still unresolved. That surprise underlines the real damage of the repressive eras in our history. For the story of *Salt of the Earth*—the strike, the film, the people—is an integral part of a tradition of progressive belief and action in our politics and in our culture, a heritage that did not completely disappear in the "haunted decade" of the fifties but went, often unwillingly, underground.

HOLLYWOOD

The film was made by blacklisted people.... They had formed an independent company on the theory that, though blacklisted, they were not going to stop making films. They would do a film outside the aegis of Hollywood and beyond its control... something that was an honest portrayal of working class life in America. —*Michael Wilson, 1975*[1]

The hearings, trials, and blacklists of the late forties and early fifties deprived hundreds, perhaps thousands, in labor, education, civil service, and the media, of their jobs. They sent some to jail and two to the electric chair. They drove some into exile and some to suicide. They struck hard at both the professional filmmakers from Hollywood and the labor union that co-produced *Salt of the Earth*. As *Salt*'s producer, Paul Jarrico, recently remarked:

...The Mine, Mill, and Smelter Workers Union was constantly under attack for being a left wing union. It was kicked out of the CIO in 1949 for being a left wing union. We were kicked out of Hollywood for the same reason. So if there was some similarity in the thinking, it was no accident.

The making of *Salt of the Earth* was a deliberate act of resistance against the repressive climate of the era, or at least an act of determination not to succumb to it.

Actually, the machinery of "McCarthyism" came into being well before the era to which the senator from Wisconsin bequeathed his name. The House Committee on Un-American Activities (HUAC) was established in 1938 under the chairmanship of Martin Dies, ostensibly to investigate "un-American" activities of both the right and the left. Both the labor movement, which had tripled its ranks in the great organizing drives of the CIO, and the entertainment industry, with its access to the consciousness of large numbers of people, came under the Committee's scrutiny at that time. In one four-day period, in 1938, 248 CIO organizers were named as Communists. In the same year, similar accusations destroyed the Federal Theater Project. Forty-two Hollywood personalities, including the eight-year-old Shirley Temple, were accused of being tools of communism before World War II interrupted the Committee's activities.

During the war the country united against fascism. Throughout the war years, labor voluntarily abided by a no-strike pledge. In Hollywood, filmmakers of every political persuasion turned out scores of patriotic films, some openly designed to enlist public sympathy on the side of our wartime ally, the Soviet Union. Since it was perfectly respectable to be pro-Soviet in those years, no one realized that a few years later films like *The North Star* (1943), *Song of Russia* (1944), *Days of Glory* (1944), and the documentary *The Battle of Russia* (1944) would become political embarrassments to their producers. During the war, political differences within the country were largely muted in the general mobilization.

The end of the war brought with it a more restive mood. In the labor movement, many of the unions, including the International Union of Mine, Mill, and Smelter Workers in the Southwest and the Conference of Studio Unions in Hollywood, mounted strikes to bring wages in line with skyrocketing prices and profits.[2] In Hollywood, too, a series of films probed critically, if not always clearly, the problems confronting American society: political corruption, juvenile delinquency, the readjustment of returning servicemen, the experience of black people, anti-Semitism. This period of social realism in Hollywood did not survive the increasingly reactionary pressures of the Cold War era.

In 1947, the Truman Doctrine, designed to contain the Soviet Union, stop the spread of communism, and protect American interests abroad, ushered in the Cold War era. The ideology of the Cold War, though rooted in the antagonism between the Soviet Union and the "free world" and in the deep-seated fear associated with the atomic bomb, provided a rationale for putting a stop to postwar militancy in the labor movement and for renewing the attack on progressive culture. One sign of the times was a series of pamphlets issued in the late forties by the United States Chamber of Commerce. Bearing titles like *Communist Infiltration in the United States: Its Nature and How to Combat It*, these reports formed the basis both for such devastating antilabor legislation as the Taft-Hartley Act of 1947 (written almost entirely by the National Association of Manufacturers) and for HUAC's new series of hearings into labor and the media.[3]

The inquisitions that began in 1947 were so devastating, so dramatically painful, that even now their excesses distort our understanding of the period itself and our vision of the years before. In the past few years, a number of studies, reminiscences, and dramatizations have focused on the blacklists—including a major Hollywood film, *The Front*, starring Woody Allen and written, produced, and directed by former blacklistees; their names and the dates of their blacklisting march proudly across the screen at the film's conclusion, as though to make amends for the past. Most of these accounts share a justifiable indignation at the shocking violation of civil liberties and the wanton destruction of human lives. Yet in dwelling on the morality play of maliciousness and idealism, cowardice and courage, presented daily in the hearing rooms and courts; in focusing on individual stories of victimization; in depicting the worst excesses of the period as aberrations tolerated by a country momentarily gripped by mass hysteria—many of these discussions offer too narrow a view. Concerned with the psychology of inquisition, they sometimes omit its economics; reacting against the era's mindless anticommunism, they ignore or minimize the role of the left.[4]

Not all the victims of the blacklists, of course, were Communists or even activists. But many of them were: an acknowledgment still awkward even today. Many of the political activists of the pre-McCarthy era remain defensive and reticent about the commitments that brought them their subpoenas. Questions about their affiliations have the ring of unpleasantly familiar charges; besides, some went to jail defending their right not to respond to such interrogation. Some who could have answered affirmatively the tired question, "Are you now or have you ever been...?" suffered a bitter disillusionment from the revelation of purges in the Soviet Union. Though some became outspoken anticommunists, others kept their disillusionment to themselves lest they give support to the right and comfort to the turncoats of the investigations. A 1976 letter to Virginia Derr Chambers (*Salt of the Earth*'s Ruth Barnes) from her daughter Linda Rageh eloquently summarizes these tangled sensitivities. Dissatisfied with the discussion after a showing of *Salt*, Rageh wrote to her mother:

> It is terrible to realize that the real complexity of the labor and left struggle cannot be communicated—partly because people... are unwilling to reexperience the bitter emotions of the past by examining them, partly because the left itself is still so precious that everyone who fought for it wants to protect it from the ignorance of those who might not understand.[5]

These sensitivities have made it hard at times to reconstruct the history behind *Salt of the Earth*, a history that some of those who lived through the blacklist era would prefer to forget. Besides, the old left, the left of the Communist Party in the thirties and forties, had always practiced a certain defensive secrecy. Most Party members simply did not talk openly about their political affiliations; and the investigations of the Cold War era, only one episode in a long history of persecution, seemed to validate their habit of silence. That habit still dies hard for many one-time Party members, even some who left it long ago.

Yet even since work on this project started, many members of the old left have begun to speak more freely and less painfully about their lives in the pre-McCarthy era. Today, some former Party members, including some interviewed for this study, regret the old lack of openness: the proliferation of "front" organizations, the use of aliases, the failure of Party members to identify themselves when working with other groups, the silencing of critical debate even within Party ranks. They believe that the atmosphere of secrecy made the Party seem more devious and threatening than it was, turning into exposures information that should have been common knowledge, feeding the paranoia that sustained the witch-hunts. They believe that the absence of open, critical discussion, rather than creating unity, finally hurt the left. Recent memoirs by Al Richmond, Jessica Mitford, and Peggy Dennis focus candidly on their experiences in the Communist Party, mingling affection, criticism, and historical insight.[6] Today, it no longer seems so shocking as it did a few years ago simply to say, yes, many of those who worked on *Salt of the Earth* once belonged to or were close to the Communist Party, and yes, the Party helped facilitate the making of the film.[7] That fact needs acknowledgment at least partly because so much mystification has surrounded it. The danger is exaggerating its significance.

The image of communism as a *bête rouge*, a powerful and diabolic conspiracy out to undermine American values and institutions, still persists in some quarters. Contemporary leftists, on the other hand, are more apt to condemn the American Communist Party (CPUSA) for its failures in revolutionary deed and vision: its emphasis during the Popular Front period (1935–39) on antifascism rather than class struggle and its consequent invisibility as a revolutionary socialist organization; its identification, except during the Hitler-Stalin Pact period in 1939–40, with the liberal reformism of the New Deal; its vigorous support of the wartime no-strike pledge; its failure to project a revolutionary ideology in the media.[8]

Somewhere between exaggeration of the CPUSA's influence and negation of its accomplishments lies the truth. In the thirties and forties a Marxist economic perspective encouraged a mlitancy in industrial trade unionism; a Marxist analysis made connections between the exploitation of workers, racial and ethnic minorities, and women; and a Marxist aesthetic insisted that art should be a weapon in the class struggle. The Communist Party was not the only leftist group around, and certainly many individuals who shared a Marxist perspective never joined any organization at all. But in those years, the Party was the major organized political expression of the progressive tendency in American life, attracting to it or to one of its front organizations perhaps as many as 100,000 Americans.[9]

The CPUSA was the logical affiliation for those who believed that socialism would provide a more humane way of life for more people than capitalism. Many who joined looked to the Soviet Union as the cradle of socialist revolution, yet many also regarded themselves, with no sense of inconsistency, as the true Americans, fighting for freedom and democracy in an age when the rise of fascism threatened both. Party members were tireless organizers on behalf of industrial workers, the unemployed, blacks, farmers, veterans. Around the Party, too, a variety of activities and organizations flourished—youth groups, athletic clubs, study groups, summer camps, housing co-ops, schools, clubs for writers and artists.

This subculture, virtually an alternative social world, had a certain legitimacy in American society as a whole.

What matters for the creation of *Salt of the Earth* is less that some of the *Salt* people belonged to the Party than that they participated in this common subculture and shared common assumptions about how society works, what is wrong with it, what they should be doing to set it right. Some of the group came originally from radical working-class backgrounds, like the sisters Zelma and Sylvia Gussin, who married Michael Wilson and Paul Jarrico respectively. The sisters' parents, sympathetic to the anarchist views of Peter Kropotkin, had worked as young immigrants in New York's garment industry. Then they had moved westward, always seeking compatible acquaintances among the scattering of socialists and Wobblies in the small towns of the Southwest, and had finally settled in California. Others in the *Salt* circle came from middle-class backgrounds, more humanistic than political; like so many other Americans, they were radicalized by depression economics at home and the rise of fascism abroad. Herbert Biberman, *Salt*'s director, graduated from Yale in drama and then worked in theaters in Paris and Moscow, returning from the Soviet Union a devotee of its theater and of its revolution. By the late thirties, most of the group had come to work in Hollywood. Not all of the *Salt* people's work in film reflected their political commitments; working in Hollywood has always necessitated a certain schizophrenia for political people. Nevertheless, there is a consistency to the texture of their lives and beliefs that helps to explain their determination to produce *Salt of the Earth* in so inhospitable an atmosphere as the early fifties.[10]

Progressives in the relatively liberal atmosphere of Hollywood in the thirties and forties led an active political, social, and cultural life. The men and women of the *Salt* circle were no exception. Sometimes they relaxed and dined with their friends at Musso & Frank's, or read, talked, drank, and argued in the rear of Stanley Rose's bookstore next door. Mostly, they worked. They gave their energies to a host of organizations over the years: the Hollywood Anti-Nazi League; the Anti-Fascist Refugee Committee; the Institute of Pacific Relations; the California Arts, Sciences, and Professions Council. They edited and wrote for left and left-liberal magazines like *Frontier*, the *Hollywood Quarterly*, the *California Quarterly*, *Masses and Mainstream*, and for the newsletters of the organizations to which they belonged. They taught in the school of the League of American Writers and organized benefits to raise money for a variety of causes. They held conferences to examine the role of the artist —focusing, as the tolerance of the war years diminished in the late forties, on ways of resisting the increasing tendency toward "thought control" in the arts.

They joined study groups where they discussed Marxist economics and Marxist criticism from the Russian theoreticians to Christopher Caudwell and Mike Gold. They talked endlessly about films and film theory, admiring (like many of their colleagues with different politics) the works of Eisenstein and of the Italian neorealists, along with American films like *Grapes of Wrath*. They deplored the evils of "white chauvinism" and imperialism. And they took "the woman question" seriously— though relegating it, like questions of race, to secondary importance after class struggle.

There was no autonomous women's movement in the thirties and forties, and women in left-wing circles often suffered from the same pervasive sexism as their sisters in more conservative environments.[11] Still, the men and women of the *Salt* circle seem to have struggled harder with this issue than leftists in other geographic areas and other sections of the organized left. Several of those interviewed for this study remember attending discussions and weekend seminars on the role of women. Sometimes, they would even argue about what feminists today call the politics of housework, though these more personal and domestic aspects of "the woman question" seemed far less significant to them than women's issues outside the home—health care, child-care centers in the workplace, and above all, the economic status of women in the workforce.

The issue absorbing the greatest share of the Hollywood left's energies was, not surprisingly, the relationship between their political commitments and their work in film. Dreaming of creating a people's art at once popular and political, they saw themselves as cultural workers naturally allied with the manual workers of field and factory, mine and mill. Herbert Biberman; his wife, actress Gale Sondergaard; and actor Will Geer had worked on the East Coast in the radical theater, so important in the cultural life of the thirties—a theater intended to arouse people to a consciousness of social injustice and a capacity for corrective action.[12] The *Salt* circle was familiar, too, with the work of leftist film groups like Frontier Films, whose superb documentaries about the lives and struggles of working people anticipated *Salt of the Earth* in some ways. The alliance the *Salt* group forged with the workers of Mine-Mill in New Mexico was unprecedented in its co-production of a feature film, but progressive labor and progressive entertainers often worked together in the years before the blacklist. Pete Seeger, Woody Guthrie, Paul Robeson, Will Geer, and others sang and performed at benefits throughout the country to entertain and raise money for the leftist unions. Cinematographer Haskell Wexler, who would later help with the secret processing of footage from *Salt of the Earth,* made films in the forties with the United Electrical Workers before becoming famous for films like *In the Heat of the Night, Medium Cool, American Graffiti,* and *Underground.*[13]

In the Hollywood film industry itself, though, integrating film and politics was more difficult, and the leftists often fought bitterly with one another about how and even if they might do so. In the Hollywood section of the Communist Party, for example, ideological combat was keen. One of the constant debates concerned the role of film content, a discussion spilling over into the Screen Writers Guild. One faction believed that since the film industry was run and controlled by monopoly capital in a capitalist society, leftist influence on film content could only be superficial. Others, like Paul Jarrico and his friend Dalton Trumbo, the first editor of the Guild's newsletter, argued that socially conscious screenwriters should stay in the industry and try to obtain more control over the films they scripted. They believed that Hollywood films would reach far wider audiences than "purer" films made and distributed independently. The blacklist, of course, made independent production an increasingly attractive option, though some blacklisted writers continued to produce screenplays for Hollywood under pseudonyms or with no acknowledgment at all— one example of the latter being Michael Wilson's co-authorship of *Bridge on the River Kwai* (1957) and *Lawrence of Arabia* (1962).

In a 1946 letter to Sam Sillen, editor of *Masses and Mainstream,* Dalton Trumbo articulated in Marxian terms his views about the proper role of the artist in Hollywood, the relation between the Guild and the industry, and the potential of film to effect social change. Many of his convictions were shared by the makers of *Salt of the Earth.* Art, they believed, should be a weapon against fascism, racial bigotry, economic oppression, and the drive toward war. The motion picture industry represents monopoly capital in control of an art form, beginning with the manufacture of the film and ending with its final exhibition. Screenwriters are "purely industrial workers under a monopoly capital set-up." To be sure, each individual writer must engage in the battle for free speech by defending his or her individual stories, but, above all, writers must organize:

> The fight for the freer use of the screen . . . rests fundamentally upon an organization basis. . . . The fight for freedom of expression is inextricably tied up with the fight for economic security. This dual battle takes the form of demands by the writer for ownership of his ideas, for free development of his scripts, for greater control of his material. It is the common fight of all labor and progressive organizations. . . . The job will not be accomplished in solitude. . . . It will be done by organized writers, striving individually and organizationally and politically in the closest possible relationship with the great masses of workers who represent the only decent, democratic, anti-fascist force in the world today.[14]

In fact, the studio system of filmmaking made it extremely difficult to introduce material that challenged the status quo.[15] Still, at least one study shows that the films of the ten men who came to symbolize the Hollywood left on trial did contain more subject matter of social relevance than Hollywood's as a whole.[16] And the presence of an articulate minority of leftists in the Screen Writers Guild, stressing the obligations of film in the battle of ideas and the role of a screenwriters' union in organizing to obtain both economic security and freedom of expression, helps to explain why the Guild was a main target when HUAC began a new series of investigations in 1947.

The 1947 hearings, chaired by J. Parnell Thomas (later himself convicted and imprisoned for mishandling public funds) resulted in the indictment of ten writers and directors active in the Screen Writers Guild, including Herbert Biberman, for contempt of Congress. They had challenged the legitimacy of the Committee under the Bill of Rights and refused to divulge their trade union and political affiliations.[17]

Hollywood at the time was facing a devastating postwar slump. Audience attendance was declining sharply—film production diminished by half between 1947 and 1948—and the increasing popularity of television spelled still greater problems in the immediate future.[18] Accusations that Hollywood was infiltrated by subversives could only aggravate matters. After an initial protest against HUAC's methods, the industry responded to the indictment of the Hollywood Ten by proclaiming somewhat paradoxically that there were no subversives in Hollywood, but that if there were they would forthwith be expelled. This policy was formalized at a meeting of producers, executives, and attorneys in the Waldorf-Astoria, called by Eric Johnston, head of the Association of Motion Picture Producers.[19] The "Waldorf Statement" pledged to fire the Ten immediately and not to rehire any one of them until he "has purged himself of contempt and declared under oath that he is not a Communist." It promised that the industry would not knowingly employ Communists; invited the talent guilds to "work with us to eliminate any subversives"; and requested Congress to enact legislation "to assist American industry to rid itself of subversive elements." This statement gave official film industry sanction to the blacklist.

The struggle of the Hollywood Ten in the courts for their rights under the First Amendment delayed further HUAC indictments for two and a half years. In April 1950, the Supreme Court refused to consider two of their cases. Soon after that, Biberman and the rest of the Ten went to jail for terms of six months to a year. In 1951, a new series of hearings produced over two hundred more blacklistees. Among them were the brothers-in-law Michael Wilson and Paul Jarrico. Wilson had won an Academy Award for the screenplay of *A Place in the Sun* and had been nominated for an Award for *Five Fingers*. Jarrico, a screenwriter for Howard Hughes's RKO, had worked steadily for fourteen years on films ranging from *Song of Russia* to *The Las Vegas Story*. "If I have to choose between crawling in the mud with Larry Parks or going to jail like my courageous friends of the Hollywood Ten, I shall certainly choose the latter," Jarrico told the newspapers on the day he received his subpoena. He did not go to jail, but he was fired that day, forbidden even to return to the studio to get his belongings. He did not work again in Hollywood for more than twenty years.[20]

Any film made by the blacklisted would have encountered opposition. Witness the remark of a lawyer for the groups who were eventually sued by the filmmakers for conspiracy to block *Salt*'s distribution. The filmmakers, he said,

> have a right to make a living. They have a right if they could to
> make a living in a shoe factory, plow factory or a hardware factory, but they didn't have a right to make a living in a sensitive in-

dustry which depended upon public acceptance of a product such as a motion picture. Their very connection with motion pictures would detract from the public acceptance of the product which the companies had to sell. Now, that being true, let's not talk about rights.[21]

Making a film at all, then, was an act of defiance for the blacklisted. But *Salt* was not only tainted by the identity of its makers, it was provocative in its content: feminist, class-conscious, pro-ethnic minority, in an era when controversy was increasingly unfashionable and even unsafe.[22]

The film world of the early fifties showed a growing reluctance to examine social issues at all. According to one study, the "social topic" film had represented close to 30 percent of total production in 1947; by 1953, at the height of the McCarthy era, that figure had dropped to 9.2 percent.[23] The darker side of the dominant mood emerged in the *films noirs*, chronicles of corruption and defeat, pervaded by a weary cynicism. The lighter side was evident in safe escapist fare—comedies, musicals, and spectaculars. Gimmickry, in those years, often substituted for content. In the theater lobbies of the nation, filmgoers received plastic lenses, one red, one green, so that they could duck the hail of arrows flying from the screen in full three-dimension. Cinerama appeared in 1952; by 1953 moviegoers could watch the martyred sufferings of Victor Mature and Richard Burton in the grandeur of cinemascope. Sensational horror films pitted body snatchers from outer space, men with X-ray eyes, and over-sexed orangutans against helpless women and brave, clean-cut young men. Responding to direct pressures from HUAC,[24] the industry made some forty films between 1947 and 1954 in which the brave, clean-cut young men did battle with the Communist menace, which was not infrequently represented by a seductive and evil woman.

When women figured at all prominently in the films of the fifties, their images ranged not so widely from saccharine to sexy: from June Allyson, Debbie Reynolds, and Doris Day to Elizabeth Taylor and Marilyn Monroe. Even those rare films featuring whole, interesting women—the occasional Katherine Hepburn movie, for example—usually presented marriage as the only happy ending, the final solution. As Marjorie Rosen put it in *Popcorn Venus*, a detailed history of women's image in film:

One of the few constants during the decade was the direction women were heading: backward.... The films which will be remembered longest...are totally devoid of females....More than ever before, "women's films" divorced themselves from controversial and timely plots and became "how to's" on catching and keeping a man....[25]

The *Salt* group kept its feminist consciousness even in this era of the feminine mystique's ascendancy. Sylvia Jarrico was writing feminist film criticism in the early fifties that anticipated many of the issues critics like Rosen would expand on twenty years later. In an article called "Evil Heroines of 1953," she pointed out that the only strong women in the films of the time were unpleasant ones; "Hollywood's sinister heroines," she wrote, "constitute a sharpened attack on the opportunities and capacities of real women to take productive action in behalf of themselves, their families, their communities, and their nation."[26]

Actress Gale Sondergaard did a one-woman show in the fifties, including readings from *Salt of the Earth*, called, "Woman, Her Emergence into Fuller Status as a Human Being in Relation to Her Mate."[27] The title, obviously related to the theme of *Salt of the Earth*, is awkward but suggestive. "Fuller status as a human being": that humanistic vision informed both the Marxism and the feminism of the group. "In relation to her mate": one senses again and again in the recollections of these men and women that the couple itself as a unit was an important working relationship, that *Salt of the Earth* was, in more ways than one, the product of interaction between husbands and wives. Though the feminism of the group stopped short of what feminists today would call radical, rarely questioning traditional ideas about love, marriage, and the family, and though it did not prevent some behavior one woman who worked on *Salt* recalls today as "plain old chauvinistic," it was genuine and important. When asked how he came to place Esperanza at the center of *Salt of the Earth*, not only as protagonist but as narrator, Mike Wilson said simply, "I never conceived of it any other way."

Determined to make films in spite of the blacklist and ironically freed from the constraints of Hollywood to make the kind of film they had always believed in, members of the group began to consider various stories for independent production as soon as the Hollywood Ten had been released from prison. These included a story on the Scottsboro boys and a treatment by Dalton Trumbo about a divorced woman who loses custody of her children when she is accused of being a Communist. Paul Jarrico, Adrian Scott (one of the Ten), and Herbert Biberman, together with movie theater operator Simon Lazarus, formed Independent Productions Corporation in 1951. The new corporation began with $35,000 in its account—$10,000 from Lazarus, the rest loans from friendly businessmen.

None of the original stories jelled for the group. Paul and Sylvia Jarrico and their young son went off to New Mexico for a vacation. They stayed, as they had the year before, at a small ranch north of Taos, a popular gathering place for progressives. Its proprietor, Jenny Wells Vincent, a collector and singer of folk and labor songs, had performed at the national convention of the International Union of Mine, Mill, and Smelter Workers. At the ranch the Jarricos spent time with a young couple they had met briefly the previous year, organizers Clint and Virginia Jencks (the Frank and Ruth Barnes of *Salt of the Earth*). On leave from a labor struggle underway 350 miles to the south, the Jenckses told the Jarricos vivid stories about the strike, some reports of which had already reached Hollywood in the papers of the left. The Jarricos visited Grant County on their way back to California. Sylvia Jarrico and the boy walked on the women's picket line; the picketers humorously advised Paul Jarrico that no men were allowed. As Jarrico tells it, he knew then that here was the story they had been looking for. The group decided that Wilson would be the ideal person to script the story. He was interested and went off to New Mexico. So the collaboration began.

In making *Salt of the Earth* in the reactionary atmosphere of the early fifties, the filmmakers had decided, as Jarrico only half-jokingly puts it today, to commit a crime to fit the punishment. Is *Salt of the Earth*, then, "Communist propaganda," as Kael and others charged? The answer is not simple, because the linkage of those two words calls up decades of clichéd response. All art reflects, implicitly or explicitly, the values of the artist; to that extent all art is propaganda. The June Allyson and Debbie Reynolds films of the fifties propagandized relentlessly for the feminine mystique. *Salt of the Earth* openly endorses equality for women and ethnic minorities and more control over their own lives for members of the working class. These were some of the main emphases of the CPUSA during the years when *Salt* was conceived and made—though members of the Party were hardly alone in sharing them. But the filmmakers did not wickedly insinuate these egalitarian doctrines into their film because they were members of the Communist Party; rather, they made the film, as some of them had joined the Party, because they believed deeply in these principles—and because they were filmmakers who wanted to work. Clearly, though, the bonds of friendship, ideology, and experience they shared over the years in the political circles of the Communist left contributed to the endurance of their commitments in the harsher political climate of the fifties.

Let Michael Wilson have the final word on the nature of those commitments. In 1953, as work on *Salt of the Earth* neared completion, he addressed the annual convention of the International Union of Mine, Mill, and Smelter Workers:

> Think back over the pictures you have seen since World War II. Can you recall one Hollywood film that deals with the life of a trade union? Can you recall one that dealt honestly with the problems of a working man or woman?...Or take the case of the Spanish-speaking people of the Southwest who comprise so important a part of your Union. Can you recall any picture that has dealt honestly with their lives and traditions and aspirations? Merely to ask this question is to answer it, and for us in this company it opened up what we felt to be a rich, untapped source of American culture. You have all heard about the revolution—3-D in Hollywood. But we felt we had a secret. We had the fourth dimension. It is called reality—the reality of working peoples' lives.[28]

NEW MEXICO: THE BACKGROUND

The older unions have deep historical roots that go beyond the period of the depression and the Wagner Act. That's especially true of the hard rock miners, the nonferrous metal miners....Because of the very conditions of their work, miners are dependent on one another, for survival, for life itself....Miners, with their own hands, take the wealth from underground. They know its value. They bring it to the top as a product. They know that without their labor it would be worth nothing, but when it comes out, all of a sudden it's worth a great deal. So they have a sense of worth, a sense of power, a sense of interconnection. They created their own union. It was built against extreme governmental and employer hostility, and it was required by life itself. — *Clint Jencks, 1975*

Grant County, New Mexico, occupies four thousand square miles in the southwestern part of the state, its terrain ranging from desert in the south to the mountainous Gila wilderness in the north. Some twenty-two thousand people—mostly Anglos, Mexican-Americans, and Native Americans—live there, half of them in Silver City, the county seat. Billy the Kid was raised in Silver City; his mother, Katherine Antrim, lies in the local cemetery. The surrounding hills are rich in minerals and full of geological wonders, like the Kneeling Nun, a large monolith overlooking the open-pit copper mines at Santa Rita. The mines of the county form an integral part of its landscape, as well as of its history and economic development.[1]

Copper is the most important of the metals mined in the region. Today thirteen hundred Grant County residents work for the Kennecott Copper Corporation alone, some of them in the open-pit mine, some in the mill and smelter nine miles to the south in Hurley. One of them is Juan Chacón, *Salt of the Earth*'s Ramón Quintero, who has worked in the Hurley smelter for the past twenty years. Chacón was the president of Local 890 during the making of *Salt of the Earth;* he is again its president today. The union hall of Local 890 is located in Bayard, about ten miles southeast of Silver City, on a circle of roads connecting the other small mining towns of the central mining district: Hurley to the south; Central, Hanover, and Santa Rita to the north and east.

At the Santa Rita mine, the second oldest copper mine in the United States, the techniques of copper mining in the Southwest were first developed. Some of the tensions of the "Salt of the Earth" strike go back almost to the mine's origins. Long a source of copper for the Mimbres Apaches, it was "discovered" in 1800 by José Manuel Carrasco, a lieutenant colonel in the Spanish army. In 1804 Carrasco convinced Don Francisco Manuel Elguea, a wealthy banker from Chihuahua, Mexico, to invest in the mine. Elguea obtained a land grant from the Spanish government and began to build a town at Santa Rita, soon a community of over six hundred. Its residents, mostly Mexican miners from Sonora, mined the copper, melted it into crude bars, and shipped it four hundred miles south to Chihuahua by mule train where it sold for sixty-five cents a pound. The miners were paid from fifty cents to one dollar a day, receiving their wages in company-issued *boletas*—paper bills that could be cashed in only at company-owned stores. Peon miners were literally wage slaves for those who owned the mines. Mexico secured its independence from Spain in 1821, but the Spaniards continued to control the mines through local designates.[2] The pattern of absentee owner and working miner—a pattern important in *Salt of the Earth*—has been called the single most important source of tension in early labor relations.[3]

Indian attacks discouraged a large-scale expansion of farming and trade, and closed mines in the area during most of the early and middle decades of the nineteenth century. But discoveries of gold and silver proved irresistible. In 1870, a group of Anglos led by one Captain John Bullard staked a claim for silver in San Vicente de la Ciénaga, once a spot where Apache hunting parties had established transient camps, then colonized in the 1700s by Spanish explorers and missionaries. The Anglos laid out a townsite and renamed the area Silver City, the model for the name change from San Marcos to Zinc Town in *Salt of the Earth*. News of Bullard's claim brought a rush of prospectors to the area, and soon the copper mine at Santa Rita, about fifteen miles east, came to life again.[4] The reopened mine, like gold, silver, coal, and copper mines throughout the Southwest, employed many Mexicans from both sides of the border. Mexican migrants contributed a knowledge of mining and smelting techniques and, in areas like Grant County, the bulk of the labor as well.

New Mexican society was hierarchic from its beginnings, its stratifications based on a sharp division between *rico* (rich) and *pobre* (poor), between *patrón* (landlord-boss) and *peón* (peasant-worker). As the *peóns* intermarried with the local Apaches, the distinctions rigidified still further. In the later nineteenth century, many of the *ricos* aligned themselves with the increasingly dominant Anglo power structure.[5]

The mining towns of the Southwest inherited the system of peonage with its class and caste distinctions. Descriptions of these towns dwell on the bitter class antagonism, a natural consequence of the companies' control over virtually every aspect of life, and on the racial animosities that divided worker from worker.[6] Mexicans constituted a majority in many of the copper-mining camps; others were "white men's camps" that refused to allow Mexicans to remain overnight. From 1875 until the late 1940s, when the International Union of Mine, Mill, and Smelter Workers won a lengthy lawsuit to bring the custom to an end, the copper companies' payrolls carried separate headings for "Anglo-American Males" and "Other Employees," systematically paying Anglo miners at a higher rate than Mexican workers (or females, Negroes, Filipinos, and Indians) for the same type of work. Some job categories were closed to Mexican workers entirely, and often they were allotted the more difficult and dangerous jobs, like extracting ore by means of the technique developed in the 1890s of caving in a large section of earth with a single blast. Like *Salt of the Earth*'s Ramón, Mexican miners often lived with dynamite and darkness, doing the jobs that spared Anglos from a similar fate.

Mexican-American families in the mining towns lived in segregated areas called "frogtown" or "jim-town" by their Anglo counterparts; no aspect of their lives escaped the corrosive touch of a discrimination that has persisted into more recent times. Juan Chacón remembers when he first started working for Kennecott:

> In the Kennecott operation we had all the Anglos checking in on one side of the time clock and all Mexican people on the other side. We had lines of pure Anglos, getting higher pay...and the change rooms were separated, the rest rooms and everything, even the eating rooms. The Mexicans were not allowed to eat with the Anglos.

And this is the voice of sixty-seven-year-old Mariana Ramírez, captain of the women's picket line in the strike that inspired *Salt of the Earth*, born in a tent because Kennecott provided houses for Anglos only:

> I've been discriminated against all my life, all my life....I've never been able to feel free....In Hurley they had the railroad tracks across the town. On the south side were the Anglos and on the north side were the Mexican-Americans. The schools were divided, one on the north side for Mexican-Americans and one on the south side for Anglos. By nine o'clock at night no Mexican could cross the tracks to the south side....I was working with an Anglo lady and we were checkers. We were doing the same thing. She was an Anglo, and she was getting fourteen dollars a week and I was getting seven....Sometimes we would work until nine

o'clock, and the manager used to go out and get some sandwiches for the secretary, who was an Anglo, and the others, who were Anglos, and not a thing for me. When I got home I was hungry, but I didn't feel like eating. Not because I was tired, but because I was hurt, from the very bottom of my heart I was hurt.

Brutal conditions in Mexico and the chaos of the revolution they precipitated drove half a million immigrants north across the border in the first three decades of the twentieth century.[7] They took jobs as farmworkers, miners, laborers on the ever-expanding network of railroads. By 1930, about 180,000 Mexican-Americans worked in agriculture, 150,000 in common labor; of the latter, more than 16,000 were employed in mining, mainly in the copper industry in the Southwest. Historians like Carey McWilliams argue that the expanding prosperity of the Southwest between 1900 and 1940 depended directly on the availability of inexpensive Mexican labor: 65 to 85 percent of the agricultural work force and 60 percent of the common labor in the mines of the Southwest.

The availability of hungry workers, the legacy of fear and resignation associated with the old system of peonage—reinforced by the feudal power structure of the company town, and the antagonisms between Anglo and Mexican-American miners made their exploitation easy and unionization difficult. Even so, the history of labor strikes and union organizing in the hard-rock mines of the Southwest extends back to the turn of the century.[8]

Early strikes anticipated the "Salt of the Earth" strike both in the demands of the workers and in the antiunion attitude and tactics of the companies and law enforcement agencies.[9] In 1915, for example, three unions of Mexican miners struck in Arizona's Clifton-Morenci copper mines, protesting the "Mexican rate" and the practice that foremen had of selling jobs to Mexicans and forcing them to buy tickets in raffles as a condition of keeping the jobs. The company sealed up the mouth of the mine with cement and told the strikers to "go back to Mexico." Hundreds were arrested, and the National Guard was called in to break the strike. Other strikes in the area in 1917-18 involved both Mexican and Anglo workers. The companies broke them up by a combination of vigilante action and the shipping of 1,186 strikers by boxcar from Bisbee, Arizona, to Columbus, New Mexico, where they were taken out to the desert and left to fend for themselves.

In many of these early strikes, the Western Federation of Miners, progenitor of the International Union of Mine, Mill, and Smelter Workers, played an active role. One of the more colorful unions in United States history, the WFM was from its inception in 1893 militant and class-conscious, arguing in the preamble to its constitution: "The working class, and it alone, can and must achieve its own emancipation" through "an industrial union and the concerted political action of all wage workers." Employers hated the WFM; some of the early strikes were settled favorably to the workers only on the condition that their locals withdraw from membership.[10] Though less active in New Mexico than in Arizona, Colorado, and Utah, the Western Federation had chartered three New Mexico locals as early as 1903. These were short-lived, but three other locals were organized in 1914, at Silver City, Hurley, and Piños Altos. Two years later, the WFM changed its name to the International Union of Mine, Mill, and Smelter Workers. During the 1920s and early 1930s, major gains in unionization for Mexican-Americans took place mostly in agriculture. Then in the mid-thirties, came the National Labor Relations Act of 1935 and the rise of the CIO. With the CIO's call to "organize the unorganized," six Mine-Mill locals were chartered in the New Mexico central mining district.[11]

Bayard old-timer Benigno Móntez, a sixty-five-year-old retired miner, still active in union affairs, remembers the difficulties of organizing in the thirties and forties:

We had to have meetings at midnight after shift work, in the little living room, the little kitchen, the little porch. There was always company officers watching to see what was going on, so we had to have the meetings in different places.... The company could not legally keep us from having meetings, but they could discharge us for any other reason.... They fought organizing.... They would say, "You've been off too much," and they'd fire you. But that was not why they fired you. They fired you because you were active organizing. Other miners kept on getting drunk and laying off and having absenteeism, but they were not active. They weren't fired. It was the active guys, the miners who wanted to improve working conditions—the company was after them all the time.

Mariana Ramírez has similar recollections:

> We had a log cabin right by the creek and this cabin was empty . . .
> they used to meet right there, underground. They didn't have any
> lights, but they had to do it because Kennecott had people spying
> on who was organizing . . . and if they ever found out, they were
> going to be fired.

Though built with such difficulty, the union movement in the area did not
for some time present a united front. The combination of company
harassment, conflict with craft unions, rivalries among the leaders of the
various locals, and ideological differences within the union sapped its
effectiveness.

In 1947, the International sent Clinton and Virginia Jencks to New
Mexico. Clint Jencks, born and raised in Colorado Springs, had been active in his union local at American Smelting and Refining Company's
Globe Smelter in Denver. He had also been active in the Communist
Party, finding in Marxism an explanation of the violence against workers
he had witnessed all his life and an analysis of the racism that attributed
local problems to "greasers" and the country's problems to the international Jewish conspiracy. For someone like Clint Jencks, whose awareness of injustice preceded but was ultimately strengthened by a theoretical
analysis of class struggle, working as an organizer in a progressive union
was "as natural as a leaf growing on a tree." Virginia Jencks was as militant as her husband. Indeed, Maurice Travis, then secretary-treasurer of
the International, recently observed rather resentfully that Virginia was
the bigger trouble-maker of the two. Like the women of the *Salt* circle in
Hollywood, she was a committed feminist, and she sometimes irritated
the male unionists with her outspoken opinions.

Militancy among the workers in the Bayard area was nothing new
when the Jenckses arrived. Clint Jencks's work as an organizer, though,
seems to have helped cement a spirit of unity.[12] Like *Salt of the Earth*'s
Frank Barnes, he received instruction in Mexican-American history, and
that history became a part of the union's fighting spirit:

> I had learned from the Chicano people things that I never was
> taught in school, about the Treaty of Guadelupe Hidalgo, that half

of Mexico had been torn off by force of arms....We used to tell the company, you don't know how easily we're letting you off. You stole this land from us. You're the interlopers. You're lucky we give you any percentage at all. We were here before you and we'll be here after you're gone.

The companies responded with growing unease, and were not at all pleased when the five separate unions in the Bayard area were amalgamated into one local, the Amalgamated Bayard District Union Local 890, on January 1, 1948.

Predictably, the companies used red-baiting to divide the workers and to enlist public opinion against the union. The union was an easy target. In 1949, Mine-Mill and ten other leftist unions were expelled from the CIO, just as the CIO had itself been expelled from the AFL eleven years earlier. Like Clint Jencks, some of Mine-Mill's officers were members of the Communist Party. Local 890 was attacked repeatedly for being part of a red union whose outside agitators were busy stirring up trouble among the peaceful, happy Mexican workers. The outbreak of war in Korea in 1950 made it still easier to equate workers' demands with Communist sympathies.[13]

Another company tactic helps explain why the "Salt of the Earth" strike went on for fifteen months. In the late forties, Jencks recalls,

We noticed that we began to have a strike every single year. But it had a pattern....We noticed that first one company would take us on—Phelps Dodge, A S & R, Kennecott—and that each strike kept getting longer. We finally found out that the reason was the employers had had an agreement, a profits pool—you take 'em one year, you the next. We'll make up the profits you lose.

Clint Jencks believes that management's recalcitrance in the "Salt of the Earth" strike grew out of the companies' joint attempt to break the district wage scale and thereby undercut the unity of the workers. "They picked one of the smaller companies as the weaker link," he says, "because it would cost very little to sustain the strike there." The companies were out to break the union; the union was out to prove that they could not succeed.

NEW MEXICO: THE STRIKE

People used to come and ask, "Who told you you could walk right there?" And we used to say, "We want to." And they'd ask, Who is your leader?" "Jane Doe." "What is your name?" "Jane Doe." Even the little girls that came with their mothers to the picket line, every time someone asked, "What's your name?"—"Jane Doe."...We were all leaders.—*Mariana Ramírez, captain of the women's picket line, 1975*

The strike on which *Salt of the Earth* is based took place in Hanover, New Mexico, at a mine owned by Empire Zinc, a subsidiary of New Jersey Zinc.[1] It began on October 17, 1950. It lasted until January 24, 1952. The specific issues were the workers' demands for portal-to-portal pay and parity in the number of paid holidays with other mines in the district. The company insisted that it would never pay for time not worked—including lunch periods and travel to and from the surface of the mine. This issue is less dramatic than the issue of safety emphasized in *Salt of the Earth*; however, safety had been paramount in other union struggles in the district. The film does accurately accentuate the underlying issues of the Empire Zinc strike: the company's arrogance toward the workers; its resistance to their efforts to negotiate their own demands; the history in the area as a whole of discrimination against Mexican-American workers; the larger struggle for power between labor and management. And it accurately portrays the central role of the women.

Even before the strike, Empire Zinc, employer of one hundred and fifty workers in mine and mill, had a reputation for being one of the toughest, most paternalistic, least responsive of the mining companies in the area. According to Clint Jencks, this strike began with "just a simple straightforward refusal of the company to follow the wage and working condition pattern...already established at the other mines in the district."[2] When the strike dragged on without resolution, he recalls,

it became obvious that the company had no intention of settling at all.... The workers...knew that what was at stake there was the right to bargain at all about their conditions of work.

A decision by the National Labor Relations Board (NLRB) in August 1951 substantiates that analysis: the trial examiner found that the strike had been called because of the company's refusal to bargain in good faith, when the union had repeatedly demonstrated a desire to resolve the issues satisfactorily. Empire Zinc, the report added, had "interfered with, coerced, and restrained its employees."[3]

For seven months, as the frustrating negotiations wore on, the strike continued more or less uneventfully. The ladies' auxiliary did its part; the women helped write leaflets, gave parties to pep up morale, participated in the union's biweekly radio program. The most visible battle between the company and the union in those months took place in the local media, each side seeking sympathy and support. EZ took out full-page ads in the Silver City *Daily Press*, attacking the credibility of the union and arguing the rectitude of its position. Members of the union and the auxiliary responded with floods of letters to the editor, some pointing out that if EZ spent as much to improve working conditions as it did on public relations there would have been no problem in the first place. Most of the letters echo the sentiments of José Carillo:

> Company untruths and propaganda are not going to settle the strike. Working conditions equal to those in the district will. (April 5, 1951)

As the film suggests, the women asserted the importance of sanitation as an issue. A pithy letter to the *Daily Press* from Anita Torres, subsequently one of the auxiliary presidents, appears with a number of letters about working conditions at EZ:

> Empire thinks us 2nd class workers. No plumbing facilities as in Anglo houses. (April 2, 1951)

But the strike remained peaceful until early June 1951.

Between June 7 and June 12, the company announced that, strike or no strike, it would reopen the mine; the picket line swelled with reinforcements; twelve picketers were arrested, including Clint Jencks and fifty-year-old Elvira Molano, *Salt of the Earth*'s Mrs. Salazar, who, like her film counterpart, had been marching with the men; and District Judge A. W. Marshall handed down the Taft-Hartley restraining order.

Those first arrests were ordered by District Attorney Thomas Foy after consultation with company officials; they were supervised by Sheriff Leslie Goforth (Will Geer's role in *Salt of the Earth*); they were carried out by twenty-four deputies requested and paid for, as Goforth later admitted to a Silver City *Daily Press* reporter, by Empire Zinc. The official charge was obstructing a "public highway"—actually a small road running through company-owned land, posted at the time with a sign saying "Private Property." The injunction meant that any miners picketing there in the future could be arrested for violating a court order. The strike almost ended that day, June 12, with a victory for the company. But that night the mining community met to decide what to do.

Salt of the Earth accurately conveys the mood of that meeting: the packed room, the heated debate, the tension, the sober silence after the affirmative vote that the women would take over the picket line. In real life, though, opposition was even stronger than the film suggests. The first vote was negative. After some discussion, the men and women agreed to vote again. This time a small majority favored the women's action. Like Ramón in the film, Juan Chacón was one of those who voted no. "I felt it was against the law," he recalls, and "it would be a hardship for the local union. I felt they had no business being in that picket line. [But] the men were finally convinced that was the only way we could win." He and Virginia Chacón, his wife and one of the founders of the ladies' auxiliary, argued bitterly over the issue, but, like Esperanza, Virginia Chacón went to the picket line.

The Silver City *Daily Press* of June 13, 1951, reports:

> In general, quiet was the rule today. Pickets still were on the march but the pickets were women and a few children. Some county officials opined that the women were not technically union members and therefore would not be affected by Marshall's order.

Originally the women's picket line was to have lasted only twenty-four hours. Mariana Ramírez, captain of the line, divided the women into two teams of eight each, one for each entrance to the mine. After the initial twenty-four hours, the community decided to extend the line as long as necessary. That turned out to be more than seven months. The chant of the line was "No les dejen pasar": "Don't let them pass." A letter from Elvira Molano in the June 19 Silver City *Daily Press* sums up the mood of the women in the early weeks of the strike. The company and the law, she writes,

> failed to realize that we women are a part of this fight. The order restrains our husbands and all members of Mine-Mill to picket, but it does not restrain us. We shall carry our fight to the victorious finish. . . . Women from over the country have joined our ranks and our picket line is solid.

Periodically the deputies attempted to break the line; the women would not be moved. On June 16, the front page of the *Daily Press* carried an eyewitness account by Bert Steele of a confrontation:

> A few minutes after 10 A.M. sheriff's deputies took red-covered tear gas grenades, held them in their hands and looked toward the picket line which consisted then of women and children. Men, many of them husbands of the women pickets, sat or moved about on the hillside above the road. . . .

> Shouts of "No les dejen!" . . . came up from the pickets and from the men on the hillside. The deputies left their cars and walked down the hot pavement. . . .

> The men on the hillside stood up and shaded their eyes against the sun, watching.

> "Don't worry," yelled a woman. "You'll get enough of us."

> The deputies began making arrests. The vacancies left by the arrested pickets were filled almost immediately with new pickets. . . .

> Suddenly a deputy let go one of the gas grenades. It skewered and rolled among the pickets, spewing the white gas and dispersing the screaming women.

> A car full of the arrested women, many of whom had children with them, moved back down the road on the way to Silver City and jail.

> The line reorganized and marched as before. The wind had blown the tear gas down the road and up the hill toward the mine.

120

A few minutes later I saw another deputy and another bomb. He walked a few yards away from me and released a bomb. The gas sprayed out, the women screamed, shaded their eyes. But the wind was blowing again, and in a few minutes the women were back at their posts.

A dusty black 1940 Chevrolet, driven by two employees of the mine, moved toward the line. . . .

The sheriff and more deputies were back again to make arrests. The cars neared the line, but the line did not move. . . .

The black Chevrolet moved into the line. Women and children seized it by the bumper and tried to move it back. Another car attempted to pass around the side of the line, but the women pushed the Chevrolet back and blocked the way. . . .

The men neared the line. They were moving faster now. Some of them were throwing rocks.

Suddenly the driver of the Chevrolet slipped it into reverse and moved back. The deputies loaded their charges into the car and drove away.

The men stood on the hillside. They held their hands straight at their sides, their fists doubled, their muscles tense. The women in the line were standing still now, not moving.

Someone among them shouted, "Form the line." Gradually the tension melted. The men moved back to the shade of a tree on the hill. The line began to move again.

Steele's report reads like the treatment for the script. One can almost hear Esperanza's voice: "But they could not break our line." As the women were arrested and herded to the deputies' cars, other women filled their places. Mariana Ramírez and her husband had taken a car equipped with a loudspeaker from community to community; by the time they returned to the line, the area was packed with cars and women.

The mass arrests on the sixteenth led to a jailroom scene much like that in the film. Fifty women and children, including twenty-nine-day-old Juan Velásquez, were imprisoned in tanks set up for a maximum of twenty-four people. The jail was not large enough to hold them all, and more than fifty others were placed under guard in two Silver City hotels. The movie does not exaggerate their spirit. From the *Daily Press*:

> There was a general air of good nature among those who Saturday were arrested after bitter struggles on the picket line. . . .
>
> "It's like a picnic," one woman commented. "We're having fun—and we're going to stay on the picket line too."

Tom Foy, the district attorney, offered to free the women if they would sign pledges to stay away from the picket line. They refused. Then he offered individual freedom to women whose relatives would post bond. Again, they refused; none would leave, they said, until all were free. Virginia Chacón vividly remembers that day, which had started with picket duty at 4:00 A.M.:

> We were in jail by 8:00 in the morning, and boy, didn't we drive them crazy. Just the way you see it in the movie. The sheriff tells us he's gonna let us go. "All you have to do is sign a little piece of paper." We all said, "BOOOOOO. We'll sign nothing for you." We said, "We'll all go together or not at all."
>
> He came about 6 o'clock and said, "Well, I'm going to take you girls home." And so we all shouted, "We're going straight to the picket line." And they hired a bus, a chartered bus. And they left us off at the picket line. Our husbands were there waiting for us. . . . A lot of them got angry [because the women had been in jail].

A party was held at the union hall that night to celebrate the women's solidarity.[4]

If ever there was joy in the struggle, those women exemplified it. They could defend themselves physically, too; when violence was directed at them on the picket line, or when scabs attempted to break through it, they did not stand by passively. Mariana Ramírez recalls zestfully:

> Everybody had a gun, except us. We had knitting needles. We had safety pins. We had straight pins. We had chili peppers. And we had rotten eggs.

The papers carry several accounts of the picketers' rebuffs of would-be scabs; rocks and chili powder in the eyes seem to have been favorite weapons of resistance, though occasionally the women resorted to hot coffee and their fists.

Clearly, though, the women were the targets of violence far more often than they were its initiators. The film downplays the extent of the violence directed at the picketers, lest its credibility be questioned. (It was, of course, questioned anyway.) In mid-July, Deputy Marvin Mosely struck fourteen-year-old Rachel Juárez, daughter of a miner, with his car, dragging her some six hundred feet; he later claimed that she had thrown herself against his fender. On August 23, several carloads of scabs tried to break the picket line. Rachel Juárez was again run down and hospitalized, this time with a dislocated shoulder. The confrontation also hospitalized Mrs. Consuela Martínez, knocked down by one car and run over by the one behind it; and sixty-four-year-old Bersabe Yguado, struck by a scab's truck that had deliberately veered her way as she sat near the road. It was this episode that brought the "guys from the open pit" at Santa Rita and "the guys from the mill" at Hurley to the scene. Over one hundred workers from Kennecott, American Smelting and Refining, and Peru left their jobs at noon when they heard about the violence and joined the women in a "protest demonstration." One of them, Augustine Martínez, was shot in the leg by one of the scabs, as Sheriff Goforth looked on.[5]

The courts made some ludicrous decisions in their determination to punish the women and the union. Carmen Rivera, threatened with a raised blackjack by Deputy Robert Capshaw, seized the blackjack and hurled it away. She was found guilty of petty larceny, fined twenty dollars and costs, and given a ten-day suspended sentence. Virginia Jencks, badly beaten by three assailants while picketing a grocery store sympathetic to the company, filed charges against them for assault and battery. They filed charges against her for "unlawfully touching another in a rude and insolent manner." They were acquitted. She was found guilty, fined forty dollars, and ordered to pay an additional twenty-three dollars in court costs.

An open letter in the *Union* a month before Christmas 1951, with the strike over a year old, gives us another glimpse of the women: "We need donations of cash, food, and clothing, especially winter clothing, for the brave women who have been holding the picket lines in freezing weather...." The response to such pleas for help was generous: food, clothing, and "the crumpled dollar bills" of working men and women poured in from locals and auxiliary chapters throughout the International —Pulaski, Tennessee; Sudbury, Ontario; Pacific Grove, California. In the Bayard area, many small businessmen extended credit generously to the strikers, at least at first.[6] But as the strike wore on, credit and tempers wore thin. There were some repossessions, and though there were no evictions in this strike comparable to the final scene in the film, many of the striking families had to leave the area to seek work elsewhere.[7]

While the women walked the picket line, a long series of legal maneuvers, obviously designed to exhaust the energies and finances of the union, was taking place in the mediation rooms and the courts. Negotiators from the union and the company met periodically and fruitlessly in El Paso. The NLRB visited the scene twice. Governor Mechem offered his services as mediator; the union accepted, the company refused. Representatives from the Federal Mediation and Conciliation Council were called in, to no avail. The courts of District Judge Marshall and Justice of the Peace Andrew Haugland ruled methodically against the union in case after case. In a three-day period in July, for example, eleven of those originally arrested were found guilty and given ten-day suspended sentences and thirty-dollar fines. Clint Jencks, the twelfth, object of special hatred as an "outside agitator" and a "Mexican lover," received a twenty-day sentence and was ordered to pay court costs. The temporary injunction became permanent, and officials of the local and the International were handed additional jail sentences and fines totaling $8,000. On June 30, 1952, the Mine-Mill publication, the *Union*, tallied up the costs of the strike. Over the course of the strike and in the litigation that continued after its settlement, fines and bails totaled $113,360. Pro-union men and women served a total of 1,148 person-days in jail.[8]

After over a year, representatives of the union and the company finally hammered out a settlement in El Paso. The union won substantial wage increases, making the hourly pay rate at Empire Zinc one of the highest in the district, and some significant fringe benefits, especially in life insurance and health and accident compensation. They also won the right of new workers to use grievance procedures during their probationary period and the right of the union to negotiate rates for new jobs. The contract renewal date at EZ was brought into line with other contract dates in the district, so that its workers could no longer be isolated as before. All strikers could return to work with full seniority rights. About sanitation

124

there seems to be no written evidence, but those interviewed unanimously agreed that not long after the strike, company-owned houses in the area got hot running water.

On the other hand, the company still had officially refused to pay for time not worked, though part of the across-the-board hourly wage in-increase was to compensate for paid holidays and portal-to-portal pay. In March 1952, Judge Marshall ordered that fines totaling $38,000 be turned over to Empire Zinc to make up for profits lost during the strike. The company continued to press charges against the strike leaders, and in September 1952, eight months after the strike had ended, six of them, originally sentenced in July 1951, went to jail to serve their ninety days. Five were released on a writ of habeas corpus on October 1. Clint Jencks, held in solitary confinement without exercise or visitor privileges, was released a week later. By then, preparations for shooting *Salt of the Earth* were well under way.

The companies never forgave Mine-Mill its intransigence. Clint Jencks in particular attracted their ire. As shooting on the film was completed, the House Labor Committee heard testimony from Richard Berresford, manager of employee relations for the Empire Zinc division of New Jersey Zinc, the "Delaware Zinc" of the film. "We are not trying to destroy this union," Berresford told the committee, "we are trying to give it proper leadership." He proposed to "catch the International Representative" whose leadership he found so objectionable.[9] Less than a month later, Jencks was one of the first labor leaders to be indicted for falsification of his non-Communist affidavit under the Taft-Hartley Act. He was convicted on the testimony of paid informer and false witness Harvey Matusow, later to have his conviction reversed when Matusow admitted lying on the stand.[10] But in the interim, Mine-Mill and Local 890 in particular devoted a great deal of time, energy, and money to Jencks's defense and to educating around the issues of the political trial.

Berresford's "We are not trying to destroy this union" to the contrary, Jencks's indictment and trial were part of the general effort to stamp union militancy out of existence. "No matter how one views the issue of communism," writes labor historian Sidney Lens of the attacks on Mine-Mill in the fifties, "no one can view with equanimity the persistent hounding of this union, the persistent attempt to 'get it'.... The conclusion is inescapable that the real target is not a few union leaders or a few unions, but the militancy and strivings of labor itself."[11] Mine-Mill could not survive the government's attacks from without, the resultant disarray within,[12] and the raids by more conservative unions on its membership. In 1967, the International Union of Mine, Mill, and Smelter Workers voted itself out of existence and merged with the CIO's United Steelworkers of America, its bitter rival for more than fifteen years.

Some of Mine-Mill's leaders during the ordeal of the late forties and fifties now argue that the long strike and the controversial film hastened the union's demise.[13] Yet it seems unlikely that the union would have survived the pressures of reaction in any case; only two of the eleven left-wing unions expelled from the CIO still exist. But the people of the New Mexican mining community earned a heightened sense of power and pride in those three hectic years at the beginning of the decade. The making of *Salt of the Earth* helped keep their story alive.

THE MAKING OF *SALT OF THE EARTH*

Preliminaries were at an end.
Resistance was about to begin again.
Now, was film-making time.
— *Herbert Biberman,*
Salt of the Earth: The Story of a Film[1]

In addition to telling the story of the struggle of working people, the process of making *Salt of the Earth* was to serve as a "cultural stimulus" for other progressive groups, demonstrating the accessibility of the film as medium and providing a deliberate model for collectivity in the production of a work of art.

Michael Wilson arrived in New Mexico in October 1951, three months before the end of the strike, and he stayed for a month. Of his presence there, Clint Jencks remembers:

Michael Wilson was just a beautiful sponge . . . he had this magnificent ability not to come in and impose what he wanted to read out of the people, but to receive. . . . In New Mexico, you wouldn't even know he was there. He was listening all the time, not talking. Everything in that film comes out of the life of the people.

Wilson returned to Hollywood to work on a treatment for the film. He completed it in the spring and brought it back to Bayard for consultation with the mining community. The decision to focus on the central relationship between a man and a woman was his; but he would proceed only with the approval of the mining families. They liked the treatment, liked the dramatic interest of the marital interaction, but insisted, in some lively and heated group discussions, on certain modifications. Scenes that did not ring true to them were excised or rewritten: "No Hollywood shenanigans," they said. Some incidents, they feared, would perpetuate negative stereotypes of the passionate Latin and the drunken Mexican. They objected, for example, to a subplot involving Ramón's infidelity with a woman whose husband has gone to Korea; it was eliminated. They objected to the characterization of Ramón as a heavy drinker, buying a bottle of whiskey with his last paycheck; Ramón as *borracho* (drunkard) came out, but the scenes in the bar, crucial in suggesting the male refuge from both work and home, remained.

This series of discussions over, Wilson returned to Hollywood to write the screenplay. He completed the first draft in early summer, the second in late August. Again there were group discussions in New Mexico, again some changes. Thus, though Wilson conceptualized and gave language to the screenplay, the entire community became involved in the complex business of shaping life into art, selecting scenes and characterizations at once typical and individual, recording the heroism of the mining community without exaggerating or diminishing it. Jarrico estimates that some four hundred people had participated in reading the screenplay by production time.

Recently Wilson commented on how the collective process worked for him as a writer:

> Ordinarily I would have detested it—because there's one fundamental axiom: that screenplays cannot be written by committee. So that if this had been in Hollywood, to have had story conferences in which I had had to please not only the producer and the director but a committee of associations . . . would have been in-

tolerable. But in this case I didn't mind it at all. . . . I welcomed their opinions because in the process of asking questions, of hearing their opinions, I was learning more about them. It made me better qualified to write the story of their lives.

His response suggests an interesting distinction between the "collectivity" of Hollywood, which too often means simply the mass production of films to suit the style of the specific studio, leaving the writer and director powerless to determine the final shape of their product, and the collaboration by consent and mutual respect in New Mexico.

Fundraising, finding locations for shooting, preparing sets, pulling together a crew, and casting the various roles continued through the summer of 1952 and the winter of 1953. The filmmakers tried to get a crew through the AFL's International Alliance of Theatrical and Stage Employees Union (IATSE), the union to which many Hollywood craftspeople belonged. That attempt was blocked by Roy Brewer, the anti-Communist head of IATSE, also chairman of the Hollywood AFL Film Council, chairman of the Motion Picture Industry Council, a moving spirit in the conservative Motion Picture Alliance for the Preservation of American Ideals, the industry's informal liaison with the American Legion, and a key figure in the precise "rehabilitation" process of public recantation required of all who had been named before an investigative committee. Brewer vowed to do everything in his considerable power to keep the film from being made.

Jarrico and Biberman persistently worked at lining up a crew. One person after another withdrew under pressure from IATSE and the studios. Of the crew finally assembled, some came from a documentary union in New York, some from television; some had been blacklisted in Hollywood. Three were blacks—an open departure from the jim crow practices of Hollywood. For many of the crew, this was their first full-length feature film.

In December, Herbert Biberman, Paul Jarrico, and Sonja Dahl Biberman, Herbert's sister-in-law, went to Bayard to prepare for the January shooting date. Though suspicious, the Silver City-Bayard establishment was not initially hostile to their presence. They brought substantial economic advantages with them, depositing an initial sum of fifty thousand dollars in a Silver City bank in the name of the International Union of Mine, Mill, and Smelter workers, Special Motion Picture Production

Account, and purchasing supplies from local stores. The filmmakers brought with them also the mystique of Hollywood, even as its outcasts. They made arrangements for housing with the owner of a local lodge. They signed a contract with a retired mining engineer, Alford Roos, to use his ranch as a shooting location; the other chief location would be a dance hall, frequented by the Mexican-American community, in Fierro, a few miles from Santa Rita.

Casting took several months. Originally, the filmmakers had not intended to cast the two main roles with local people. Everyone assumed the role of Esperanza would be played by Gale Sondergaard, a veteran of Hollywood films. For the part of Ramón, the filmmakers drew up a contract with Hollywood actor Rodolfo Acosta, only to have him withdraw under pressure from the studios. The second choice for Ramón was an Anglo Hollywood actor, one of the blacklisted. Indeed, one of the purposes of the film was to provide work for some of the blacklisted. Soon, however (and if Virginia Chacón is accurate, with a little prodding from the mining families), the filmmakers realized that to fill the roles with Anglos would be to perpetuate a blacklist older than the one that had evicted them from Hollywood. Gale Sondergaard gracefully relinquished the role of Esperanza. Still, they were convinced that professionals rather than community people must play the major roles. Rosaura Revueltas, the recipient of two awards for her performances in Mexican films, agreed to play Esperanza.[2] But no professional Mexican actor seemed right for Ramón. Finally, after a long search and with grave doubts on the part of Herbert Biberman, Juan Chacón, the newly elected president of Mine-Mill Local 890, got the part—his main advocates Rosaura Revueltas and Sonja Dahl Biberman.

Casting some of the other roles also presented problems, problems treated seriously by both the Hollywood and the New Mexico contingents. Sometimes jealousies flared as real-life husbands were cast opposite others' wives. More seriously, no one wanted to play the mean Anglo deputies; the Rockwell brothers, who looked the part—tall, slim, fair, lean-hipped, and twangy-voiced like the real-life deputies—finally agreed but feared, with some justification, that their union friends would confuse art and life if they performed the hated roles too convincingly. It took several community meetings to resolve the issue. Biberman records a process of gentle persuasion. Clint Jencks remembers simply, "We had to break their arms to get them to play those parts."

A production committee had been set up even before the arrival of the crew. Michael Wilson, addressing delegates at the 1953 convention of Mine-Mill about the making of *Salt of the Earth*, described the committee's origin and functions:

> For the first time in the history of motion pictures a group of film technicians and a labor union had come together to make a major film. We tried to make this symbolic unity a living thing by setting up a production board composed of four members from the company, four members from the union, four from the auxiliary. This group of twelve made up the policy body during the course of this production, handled matters ranging from transportation, supply, babysitting, feeding of cast and crew, to questions of policy in the content of the film.[3]

The production board coordinated the whole complicated business of making a film on location. The union's spirit and sense of organization, developed during the strike, carried over into its work on the film; and such mechanisms as the union radio program and the roving truck with loudspeakers, no longer needed to call people to the picket line, now called out the days' needs for extras and announced the locations for shooting instead. Predictably, the members of the ladies' auxiliary assumed a major share of responsibility for the daily maintenance problems of child care, food, transportation, communication. One of the Hollywood people who worked with them on these tasks was Frances Williams, a black woman from the Hollywood political community. Her presence seems to have been particularly valued by the women of New Mexico, one of whom said, "Don't forget to talk about Frances; she always gets left out."

Shooting began on January 20, 1953. A forty-page chronology prepared by Paul Jarrico in 1955, documenting for Independent Production Company's lawyers the systematic opposition to *Salt of the Earth*, carries the entry:

> Jan. 20, 1953 thru Feb. 9, 1953—Shooting continues. . . . Equipment inadequate . . . but relations with Mine-Mill brothers and sisters as well as the general community are excellent and steady progress is made.

130

That progress was soon disrupted. Jarrico's chronology details what happened next:

> Feb. 9, 1953—First press attack. Lead item of the gossip column of the *Hollywood Reporter* (widely read in the motion picture industry) says:
>
> *"H'wood Reds are shooting a feature-length anti-American racial issue propaganda movie at Silver City, N.M. SAG Prexy Walter Pidgeon got the tip in a letter from a schoolteacher fan in N.M. Pidge immediately alerted FBI, State Department, House Un-American Activities Committee, and Central Intelligence Agency."*
>
> Feb. 12, 1953—Second press attack. Victor Riesel, in a column syndicated throughout the country . . . reports we are shooting
>
> *"not too far from the Los Alamos Atomic proving ground. . . . Where you try to hide secret weapons . . . you find concentrations of Communists. . . . Tovarisch Paul (Jarrico) brought two carloads of Negroes into the mining town. Soon they were deployed for their first shooting—a sequence which starts with mob violence against them."*
>
> . . . Letter dated Feb. 12 from Pathé informs us they will no longer process our film.
>
> Feb. 13, 1953—AFL Film Council issues public attack, carried in trade press in Hollywood and in press and on radio nationally. Roy Brewer quoted widely as council chairman:
>
> *". . . Hollywood has gotten rid of these people and we want the government to investigate carefully."*
>
> Feb. 10 thru Feb. 22, 1953—Increasing repercussions in the Bayard area of the press and industry attacks. Local theatre owners refuse to continue private projection. . . . Workmen's compensation insurance policy cancelled. . . . Our accountants . . . notify us they will no longer handle our business.
>
> Feb. 24, 1953—Inflammatory speech by Congressman Donald Jackson [D., Calif.] in the House:

"...I bring to the attention of the Congress, and through it to the American people, some facts regarding a picture now being made under Communist auspices in Silver City, N.M....This picture is being made...not far from...Los Alamos [by] men and women who [are] part of the pro-Soviet secret apparatus in this country.

"...This picture is deliberately designed to inflame racial hatreds and to depict the United States of America as the enemy of all colored peoples...I shall do everything in my power to prevent the showing of this Communist-made film in the theaters of America...."

Feb. 25, 1953—Immigration investigators...arrest Rosaura Revueltas.

Mar. 3, 1953—In Bayard: At 1:30 A.M. four or five bullets are shot into Jencks's unoccupied car. During day, mob stops shooting of street scene outside Union hall, knock over camera, punch members of crew and cast....

That evening, vigilante meeting in American Legion Hall in Central issues ultimatum to staff and crew: leave area by noon of next day 'or be carried out in black boxes.'

Mar. 6, 1953—Businessmen in Silver City and Bayard area demonstrate their "Americanism" by closing up a shop for two hours to see anti-Communist movies. Shooting concluded....

No one connected with *Salt of the Earth* had anticipated so vicious a reaction. The final days of shooting took place under near-siege conditions, with the state highway patrol guarding the roads to protect cast and crew. After the filmmakers' departure on March 7, the home of Floyd Bostick, the film's Jenkins, and the Mine-Mill union hall in nearby Carlsbad were burned to the ground.

These accelerating pressures resulted in some ellipses, some mismatches, some inclusions of poor footage, some patches of bad sound that still embarrass the filmmakers today. They also necessitated some interesting stratagems. After Revueltas's arrest and "voluntary" deportation, some of her remaining scenes were shot using a double; others were shot in Mexico, illegally. As Mike Wilson puts it, "We finally fell on a device...

in which a test would be shot of Rosaura for a future film...and this was permitted. And it just so happens that the tests that we chose to do were a couple of the missing scenes." It was in Mexico, too, that Esperanza's voice-over was recorded. One sequence, the shouts announcing the eviction, was filmed at Will Geer's ranch in Topanga Canyon with volunteer extras from Los Angeles's Chicano community.

Through all this harassment, the relation between the professional filmmakers and the union families continued to be good. Both groups are full of anecdotes about the experience of making the film together. They remember the hard-won transformation of Juan Chacón from an awkward amateur to a first-rate actor; the cooperative set construction under the guidance of blacklisted chief grip Paul Perlin and blacklisted carpenter Bob Ames; the evening rehearsals after the day shift at the mines was over; the sometimes stormy production board conferences before almost every scene; the laughter and high spirits that accompanied a successful take; the mounting sense of pressure and danger. Biberman's book pays special tribute to the women of the community, always ready

> to act as technical advisers, to leap into any scene that required background people, to provide audience and encouragement, to ...keep our courage high when our thin, middle-class patience showed holes. Mrs. Chávez, Mrs. Flores, Mrs. Espinosa, Mrs. Iguado. And...the serious, gay, true and beautiful artists: Angy [Angela Sánchez], Clorinda [Clorinda Alderette], Henrietta [Henrietta Williams], and Virginia [Virginia Jencks]. (p. 77)

Not that the interaction between the two groups was conflict-free. Given the differences between them in class, race, and background, some tensions were inevitable. Occasionally the filmmakers felt misunderstood. Occasionally the union people felt patronized. The union families wondered why the people from Hollywood would not share their homes. To the Hollywood group it was obvious that they could not adequately communicate with one another if they were scattered among three villages. Herbert Biberman's dramatic and authoritarian temperament sometimes antagonized people in both groups. Perhaps the most enduring source of tension was the casting of Rosaura Revueltas in the central role. No one in New Mexico questioned the brilliance of her performance as Esperanza, but it rankled then and still rankles today that this crucial part went to a woman outside the New Mexican community. On that issue the professionalism of the Hollywood group took priority over collective decision-making.

The only conflict which finally proved irreconcilable, though, was an artistic disagreement among the professional filmmakers themselves: between the Hollywood group and Leo Hurwitz, the documentary film-maker from New York's Frontier Films, a blacklistee who had been invited to New Mexico as consulting director. Hurwitz wanted far more footage for raw material than the Hollywood group was willing (or felt able) to shoot. He was committed to greater subtlety and variety than Biberman's simple, stationary camera-work would allow.[4] Hurwitz soon left New Mexico and went back to New York, irritated at the disregard of his advice. His young assistant, Joan Laird, stayed behind and kept working; on the last day, she and Will Geer smuggled some of the footage, along with a few plants for Geer's Topanga Canyon nursery, across two state borders to Los Angeles.[5]

A great deal of work remained before the disparate pieces of celluloid could become a finished film. Two documents vividly describe the embattled effort still ahead. One, a letter from Howard Hughes that originally appeared in the Congressional Record, outlines for Congressman Jackson the steps necessary to finish the film and ways to prevent its completion and distribution; the other, Jarrico's chronology, is a stark record of fact that brings home the full destructiveness of the blacklist era. Excerpts from both are in the last section of this book.

Yet the union families and the professional filmmakers parted with a sense of accomplishment. On the whole, in spite of the occasional tensions, the collaboration in New Mexico had proceeded not only smoothly but happily. Almost all the people interviewed for this study recall the experience—its intensity, its camaraderie, its purposefulness—as one of the high points of their lives. Some of them believe that the healthy collaboration was possible precisely because the Hollywood people and many of the union families shared a common political situation, a common belief in the significance of this particular project, a common ideology that emphasized the equal value of all work. The filmmakers brought their technical expertise, their knowledge of their craft; the union families, their experiential knowledge, their resourcefulness, their "people power." Both groups developed a deep and enduring respect for one another, as hard and capable workers and as dignified, decent human beings.

Though the material differences in lifestyle between the "cultural workers" from Hollywood and the mining families of New Mexico were (and still are) very real, the joint effort on *Salt of the Earth* depended on a productive give-and-take across barriers only rarely bridged in this society. Some of the friendships formed then have lasted over the years.

WE, THE WOMEN

Come whatever would come, we the women made a motion that we would take the line. —*Braulia Velásquez, at the Forty-Seventh Convention of the International Union of Mine, Mill, and Smelter Workers, Nogales, Arizona, 1951*[1]

And what of the women of the New Mexican mining community? We know that they performed heroically on the picket line, that they developed a spirit of unity, that their participation involved not only courage, but humor and joy. We know that neither the strike nor the film could have happened, let alone succeeded, without them. But to what extent did the rejection of the "old way"—the time-worn definition of sex roles, the assumptions about proper conduct for women—carry over into the daily life and ongoing consciousness of the community? The question has no easy answer. The gradual growth in strength and self-worth for the women, the gradual if qualified acceptance of their participation by the men, were real; still, the real story is less clear, more ambiguous, more diverse, than the steady, structured progress of the women's community in the film.[2]

When I went to New Mexico in 1975, I half hoped to find a little enclave of liberated women and men, equal partners in life. Of course that simplistic expectation was disappointed. The Bayard community was not exempt from a process feminist historians have often observed: at times of crisis, women emerge from their homes to perform work demanding reservoirs of strength, courage, and skill, and sex roles become less clearly defined; in periods of normalcy the "old way" reasserts itself.

In New Mexico, the "old way" was reinforced by the limited options for the women of the strike. They were, after all, miners' wives, with few opportunities for work outside the home. Their militancy on the picket line had little to sustain it once the men were back on the job and the women back in the house. Yet Clint Jencks's summary also rings true: the people of New Mexico "slid back into the old way," he concedes, "but not all the way back."[3]

The New Mexico community has always had its share of activist women—those who, like Mariana Ramírez, had been involved early in organizing. But most of the women had lived traditional lives as full-time homemakers, mothers, wives.[4] The Catholic Church, a powerful influence in the community, confirmed the patriarchal social structure. During the strike, for example, the priest of the Hurley diocese warned the women to go back into their homes lest they sin.[5] Left at home with their frustrations, with no feminist ideology to explain their lives and their feelings, the women often resented their husbands; like Esperanza, they sometimes resented the union itself. Clint Jencks describes the gulf of misunderstanding that separated the women from the men when he arrived in 1947, a gulf firmly established in the opening scenes of *Salt of the Earth:*

> In general the women were almost in opposition to the union because of the way that the men had used it very often as an excuse to get out of the house, to go off to the bar.... We needed unity among the workers.... I found out that we didn't even have unity in our families. The women would have the responsibility of taking the meager paychecks and trying to spread them over all the needs of the household and the kids.... All of a sudden the man comes home from work one day and says, "We're gonna strike. There's gonna be no income." He hasn't discussed this with his wife—what are the problems on the job, or why are we fighting and will you help.... Well, you wouldn't ask help from a woman anyway.... What would naturally be the reaction of a woman when she's been excluded? She's got the whole responsibility; the man doesn't even conceive of the problems because he's separated himself from all the problems of managing on his salary.... I moved from thinking it was a union struggle to realizing it was a struggle of the whole people.

On the whole, the women's concerns and those of their husbands seemed to lie in different worlds.[6] To bring the women and men together the local adopted some new strategies. In most communities the union newspaper went to the union hall; Local 890 had it delivered to the homes, where the women could share it. The local invited the women to come to the union hall, and gradually it became a social gathering place. On Friday nights it was packed with eager bingo players competing for prizes solicited from local merchants: groceries, furniture, lamps, chairs. On Saturday nights there were socials or movies—a Charlie Chaplin film, some comics, a movie from distributor Tom Brandon. Soon some of the women began going to union meetings with their husbands. Virginia Chacón reflects on the transition:

> We asked the men to bring their wives, and sometimes they wouldn't, and we'd go visit the lady. And she'd tell us why she wouldn't participate—that her husband would say that ladies shouldn't belong to an organization—just do women's things. So we'd talk to her, and finally we'd convince her....

> I felt that if Johnny was going to be active in the union, why shouldn't I? What's good for the goose is good for the gander. We felt that the union is not for the men only, it's our union too.... We felt that if our husbands were going to belong to the union, we should do something about it too.

Virginia Chacón, Virginia Jencks, Mariana Ramírez, and several other community women decided to form a ladies' auxiliary chapter. The phrase "ladies' auxiliary" today conjures up images of women subordinate to their wage-earning husbands, gathering to extend in harmless sociable ways the home's domestic functions and women's supportive roles. There is some truth in the image. Like most auxiliaries, Bayard No. 209 first emerged as a support group for the men.[7] Still, the auxiliary meant that for the first time the women had an organization that was theirs, a time and place for meeting, and a structure for participating in an organized way in issues and struggles of concern to the community as a whole. Trivial though sewing circles and enchilada suppers may sound in retrospect, they provided an evolutionary step toward a more self-conscious women's culture—the slow, necessary groundwork for the more dramatic entrance of the women into the activist arena in 1950, in the struggle that did change, at least for a time, the consciousness of the community about women's issues.

With encouragement from the International, the women of the Bayard area formed Mine-Mill Auxiliary Chapter No. 209 in 1949. Virginia Chacón remembers going from house to house with one or two others, soliciting membership; "and some of the ladies," she adds, "didn't have to be asked. They'd come by themselves." Many of the husbands disapproved, suspicious of this awakening interest in things outside the home.[8] Family arguments were not infrequent. Undaunted, the auxiliary began to meet on the second Thursday of every month. As the strike against Empire Zinc wore on, month after month, the participation of the women escalated. Not only did they raise funds, distribute leaflets, and speak on the radio program, they also voted to send several representatives from the auxiliary to every Local 890 executive board meeting: auxiliary president Daria Chávez, vice-president Chana Montoya, Corrine Rivera, and Selsa Majalca. When the Taft-Hartley injunction came, the women were ready to act.

Historians have increasingly paid attention to the contributions of women organizers like Mother Jones and Mother Bloor and to the militancy of women workers in the fields and factories. They have paid less heed to the role of women's auxiliaries in predominantly male unions. The spirited and sustained activism of the Bayard women deserves a special place in women's, labor, and Chicano history. But this struggle had its antecedents and parallels, both in the progressive unions of the thirties and in Mine-Mill itself around the time of the "Salt" strike. This tradition of women's militancy, alive in the hearts of women like Virginia Chacón and Virginia Jencks, helped shape and sustain the struggle in New Mexico.

In 1952, Dorothy McDonald, who chaired Mine-Mill Women's Auxiliaries in the early fifties, described the growth of a number of Mine-Mill auxiliary chapters and recounted their participation in various union struggles, both against the companies and against the raids of the CIO's Steelworkers into Mine-Mill territory. Her article suggests a pattern of development applicable in New Mexico: at moments of stress, during strikes against recalcitrant companies, or at moments of greatest pressure from more conservative rival unions, the auxiliaries would spring to life, either securing a charter for the first time or greatly expanding their membership. McDonald's report lists the tasks performed by the auxiliaries without embarrassment or apology for "women's work"—staffing the "coffee-kitchen" and the strike benefit office; organizing entertainments—plays, concerts—with local talent; handling the distribution of "Christmas cheer"; organizing sewing centers where clothing was repaired and distributed to the families of those on strike; acting as midwives and nurses for the pregnant and the ill. With similar pride and no sense of contradiction, she records other, less predictable functions performed by the women: physically preventing rival organizers from visiting Mine-Mill members to pressure them into changing their affiliation; writing and performing radio scripts during strikes; protesting to government officials against the Taft-Hartley and McCarran acts; lobbying the Wage Stabilization Board to break through the wage freeze; and occasionally engaging in pitched battle. At a strike in East St. Louis, for example, around the same time as the New Mexico strike, an auxiliary was organized in a morning to resist a "back to work" movement. The women

> broke up the opposition move after about one hour of keeping them surrounded and telling them what was good for them. The strike was seven months old at that time, and no doubt would have been broken that day had it not been for the militant spirit of those women.[9]

If one turns back to the thirties, the examples multiply. Many of the CIO unions had active, militant women's auxiliaries which participated regularly in strikes. Documents like the "First Annual Report" of the Illinois Women's Auxiliary, Progressive Miners of America (1933)[10], by auxiliary president Agnes Wieck, bear out the generalization. Militant, feminist, and class-conscious, this report insists that the auxiliary "should have a voice in those questions that involve the very lives of our women and children," complaining that "in matters of policy, the auxiliary officials have been regarded as outsiders by the officials in our men's union." It strikes out explicitly at the stereotype of the auxiliary:

> Social affairs and raising of strike relief are among our numerous activities, but these things are not the end and aim of this Auxiliary.... In that first Convention we recognized the class struggle.

139

We advocated labor legislation, labor education, a youth movement, independent working-class political action, and pledged ourselves against all wars. We declared ourselves an integral part of the labor movement. We dedicated our lives to the struggle for bread and freedom.

It describes some episodes that anticipate the events of the Bayard strike:

We told our men to go home and mind the children, we were going to the aid of our sisters of the auxiliary....On the Taylorville picket line mothers...were met with bayonets of soldiers. Choked with tear gas, jabbed by bayonets, the women hurled their defiance at the military power.

The women of the coal fields, it says,

have lost their shyness, their timidity, their feelings of inferiority. They preside over meetings, keep books, write records, letters, news reports, form committees to visit public officials, mount improvised rostrums to take their turns at spellbinding.[11]

Twenty years later the women of Bayard would repeat that experience.

In the course of their months on the picket line, the women of the central mining district seem to have earned the surprised respect of most of the men and to have developed an increasingly high assessment of their own capabilities. The men obviously took a great deal of pleasure in telling the courts and the media, as Ramón tells the sheriff at the end of *Salt of the Earth*, that the women are now running the show. Ernest Velásquez, vice-president of Local 890 during the strike, was quoted in the Mine-Mill *Union*:

We asked our wives if they thought we should knuckle down and give up the strike. They told us, "Hell, no, you guys go home and mind the kids and clean the house and wash the dishes. We're taking over this strike. We'll not give up now." And that's what we fellows did. And that's what our wives did.

In 1953 Angel Bustos, rank and file member of Local 890, told the annual convention of Mine-Mill, "You will see in *Salt of the Earth* that we don't count very much on the women and neither did the bosses, but when the ladies take over the picket line and help the workers in the struggle, like we had in New Mexico, you will see what women can do."[12]

The cooperation and mutual pride emerge in stories like the one in the Silver City *Daily Press* of August 3, 1951, "Women Are among El Paso Negotiators." The front page has a picture of the negotiating committee: Pablo Montoya, Ernest Velásquez, Carmen Rivera, Catalina Barreras, and Elvira Molano. The Mine-Mill *Union* announced, "Three of the most active women leaders have been elected to full membership in the official bargaining committee for the Empire Zinc strikers....The three women were a part of the negotiating committee which traveled to El Paso a week ago for another vain attempt to bargain with the company." Cipriano Montoya, Local 890 president, is quoted as saying that "the women have earned the right by two months of around-the-clock picketing at Empire Zinc; by standing up to arrests, jailings, gunmen, blackjacks, and tear gas."[13] The participation by women on an official union negotiating team was a significant change in the status quo. And that women and men who were not married to one another should travel on business to another place where they had to stay overnight was a departure from custom that heralded a new freedom for women.

Yet this optimistic account requires some qualification. In addition to reflecting real pride and respect, the union's insistence on the women's independence was also practical: if the women were autonomous, the men were not liable for breaking the injunction. Besides, their role made good press. Finally, the leadership of the International, to do it credit, believed strongly in bringing the women into the struggle, but perhaps less to improve the lot of the women themselves than to create a unified class consciousness. Virginia Chacón does not believe that the women ever seriously influenced the real decision-making of the union. When the final negotiations took place, no women were included among the union members who worked out the terms of settlement; clearly some tokenism was involved in the women's participation in the July negotiations, when there was little hope of settlement.

The "dancing dog" syndrome underlies many of the men's statements about the women's performance. The contradictions in an article by José Fuentes, president of Local 903 in El Paso, Texas, written for the *Union* after a visit to the picket line, reveal much about the ambivalent attitudes of the men and the strength of traditional assumptions about women's roles:

141

> Among the seven of us...who went to visit the strikers, none of us had thought to find such high morale. We would never have thought it possible that the wives of the striking brothers would have felt such a sense of responsibility and cooperation or that they would have had such an urge to struggle jointly with their husbands, fighting for a life a little more comfortable for themselves and their children.

> ...They knew that the responsibility rested on them—the responsibility that, because of technical questions of law, had been lifted from the shoulders of their husbands. And when they saw that the future of their homes hung in the balance, thinking only of the welfare of their children, nothing else mattered to them.

> Jail, clubs, pistols, tear gas, criticism, blows from the deputies, every kind of inhuman treatment—all turned out to be nothing, compared to the happiness of their homes.

Somehow in the midst of this eulogy, the women Fuentes had begun by praising as "veteran fighters" become first and foremost the guardians of the home. Fuentes would be surprised to know that some of the gaiety on the picket lines came from the women's delight in taking an active part in a struggle that certainly included the welfare of the home but that took them blessedly out of the house. *Salt of the Earth* accurately records the men's ambivalence. Esperanza's line, "I think they were afraid. Afraid the women wouldn't stand fast. Or maybe afraid they would," says volumes.

The making of *Salt of the Earth* undoubtedly focused and honed the consciousness that had been forged in the strike itself. "The old way" is a term from the film; some of the people in New Mexico still use it as a way to talk about the problem. But they do not always agree.

> **Virginia Chacón:** We're still back in the old way. Not the new way....The movie was made, fine. That's as far as it got. We went back to the old way. And it's still in existence.

> **Mariana Ramírez:** Ever since in our community there is a certain respect for the ladies.

Both of these statements are true. The first addresses the daily realities of women's lives; the second, consciousness. And consciousness can embrace some contradictions. A man can respect his wife as a capable human being full of potential creative energy and still believe in his heart that she was destined to do the dishes.

One year after the women took over the picket line, the union gave a party in honor of the auxiliary. The filmmakers from Hollywood were there, too. The women relaxed, listened to speeches in their honor, and gave some speeches of their own. The men did the cooking, serving, and cleaning up. It was a gesture, of course. No such dramatic role reversals took place in the homes. Still, the women interviewed for this study believe that in the two or three years immediately following the strike, things were different, both in the home and in the union. They remember that some of their husbands took on more of the housekeeping and child care than they had in the past. They remember a greater male sensitivity about including the women in discussions on issues outside the home. Women appeared at union conferences and conventions as spokespersons for Local 890: Dora Lucero and Belén Vallegos went to Denver; Virginia Chacón went to Nogales; Anita Torres traveled to Canada, where she told the story of the strike and of the subsequent Taft-Hartley indictment of Clint Jencks to union audiences in Kimberly, Vancouver, Copper Mountain, and Brittania.

But the old way began to reassert itself. The women were tired after the strike, exhausted both by the emotional drain of the struggle and by the conflicts with their own men. The making of the film seems to have brought some of these conflicts into sharper relief, though finally it is impossible to sort out what changes were wrought by the strike itself and what by the filmmaking that followed. Today, the women tell of broken marriages that could not endure the strain, as well as of relationships that moved to a new level of sharing and understanding. Mariana Ramírez and Anita Torres believe that their own marriages became more egalitarian partnerships after the strike. Others say it made no difference at all.

One incident testifies at once to the power of the strike and the film to have raised consciousness about the significance of women's issues and to the limitations of such consciousness-raising. At the Forty-Ninth Convention of Mine-Mill, when *Salt of the Earth* was nearing completion, Dorothy McDonald rose and read to the gathered delegates what amounts to a women's plank of eleven resolutions.[14] It began with five "whereases":

Whereas, the International Union of Mine, Mill, and Smelter

Workers is the organization of workers in an industry almost entirely employing men, and

Whereas, men cannot be wholehearted union members without the cooperation of their womenfolk; and

Whereas, women constitute an important and at times decisive section of the people of our various communities, and our union needs their understanding, sympathy, and support to guarantee its future growth and solidarity in these days when the labor movement is under such vicious attack; and

Whereas, there are many areas of union activity in which women have a special interest, e.g., safety, health, compensation, political action, housing, education, child welfare, etc.; and

Whereas, women are people . . .

The scope and vision of the statement in its entirety are remarkable. It recognizes that the union should encourage the support and participation of the women not only because it will be useful for the difficult times ahead, but because it is right. It acknowledges that certain issues are of particular concern to women; among those issues it includes political action as well as child care and education. It insists that the International give special attention to the role of ethnic women—black and Mexican-American. It urges support for a publicity campaign for *Salt of the Earth*, spearheaded by local women. And it argues that the all-male union must do more than simply pay lip service to the idea of women's participation in the life of the union; the International and the locals should give concrete support: a special section for women in the *Union;* a paid organizer for the auxiliaries. The resolutions, supported eloquently by men and women at the convention, passed by voice vote.

Few were vigorously implemented.[15] In New Mexico and for the union as a whole, other issues moved into center stage, replacing the "woman question" as matters of concern. In the recession that followed the Korean War, the bottom dropped out of the zinc market, and most of the lead-zinc mines in the state were closed. Hundreds of families lost their jobs. In Grant County, every lead-zinc mine in the area stopped operations. At the same time, the purges and trials of labor leaders struck hard at Mine-Mill's leadership, and the union devoted its most militant efforts to resisting the tide of antileft and antilabor legislation and prosecutions.[16] In spite of the continued militancy of some of its members—including a faction in Local 890—Mine-Mill was forced to join the trend toward "mainstream" unionism, culminating in the merger in 1967 with the United Steelworkers of America.

On the whole, feminist militancy petered out in those years as well. The fifties did not provide a hospitable climate for strong women. Nor were all the male unionists in Mine-Mill and the other leftist unions pleased about the emphasis on feminism. To Clint Jencks, some of them complained, "Why did you have to bring in the woman question? Why couldn't you have made a straight labor film?" Equality may be indivisible, but each struggling group has its priorities.

In recent years, as the result of a renewed struggle, this time over Kennecott Copper's firing of Juan Chacón, again president of Local 890, and treasurer Israel Romero, there have been some sporadic attempts to revive the auxiliary. So far they have been largely unsuccessful. Life is easier now in Grant County than it was twenty years ago. Living conditions are better, at home and on the job. Kennecott has the reputation of being a good place to work. Most of the homes, Anglo and Mexican-American, have indoor toilets and hot running water. The sharp edge of anger in much of the community, among both men and women alike, has gone blunt.

More women work outside the home—mostly in clerical jobs, but a few as truck drivers, crane operators, smelter workers. They need not function in auxiliaries in order to assert their influence on the larger society. Juan Chacón believes that things have changed, that women and men now see one another in more egalitarian ways. His daughter Esperanza (named after the Esperanza of *Salt of the Earth*) is the secretary for Local 890 in Bayard. More militant than some of the union men, she seems at home among them.

But one is left somehow with the image of Virginia Chacón. Strong, intelligent, courageous, she lives with her husband some twenty miles from the Bayard area, on the other side of a ridge of mountains in the Mimbres River Valley, on a plot of hand he inherited from his grandfather. Chacón's mother lived with them until her recent death, too ill to care for herself. His father, an aged man who speaks no English, lives nearby. There is no phone, and Chacón drives the only car to work. Esperanza Chacón Villagrán and her husband live down the road in a mobile home. She leaves her young son with her mother when she goes to the union hall. Virginia Chacón stays at home and takes care of the baby.

When Juan Chacón told me how much better things had become for the women, she said to him, "Look at your own home. What about me?"

It seems legitimate to conclude that the rigid definition of sex roles did become more flexible in the months and even years immediately following the strike and the making of the film. The status of the women in the area, in terms of the kinds of jobs open to them, the options in lifestyles available, has improved over the years—probably less as a result of the strike or the film alone than as a result of the demands of the more recent feminist and Chicano movements. In spite of these changes, the "old way" has shown a greater tenacity than seemed likely at the time; but a heritage of awareness about a "new way" remains. A heightened consciousness is hard to maintain, however, apart from a specific situation to sustain it and can be more painful than ignorance if there is no productive way to use it. The feminist struggle may be the longest one of all.

SALT OF THE EARTH: A CRITIQUE

> *Salt of the Earth* is a piece of art that . . . tries to project how, within the crucible of the old life, new cultural forms come into being.
> —*Ellen Cantarow,* The Radical Teacher, *1976*[1]

Though intricately related to history, *Salt of the Earth* is not itself history, it is art. Nor is its art that of the documentary. As even a quick reading of Michael Wilson's literate screenplay suggests, the film carefully shapes, selects, and synthesizes characters and episodes. Not every incident in the film happened in this particular strike; obviously not every incident in the strike went into the film. *Salt of the Earth* deserves consideration for what it is: a finished work of film fiction.

Some contemporary critics, including some sympathetic to its vision, have dismissed *Salt of the Earth* as being old-fashioned, sentimental, melodramatic, linear, "Hollywoodish." Radical film critics today argue that instead of drawing viewers into its illusionary world and asking them to suspend their disbelief, film should call attention to itself as a medium by ironic disjunctures betwen image and sound track, by dislo-

146

cations in time, by startling juxtapositions in image; it should create a critical consciousness in audiencs rather than appeal simplistically to their emotions. Radical film art today is supposed to be evocative, ambiguous, forcing viewers to question their very assumptions about the existence of a rational social order. The overt ideological content of a work, according to this school of thought, matters less than that its form challenge our habitual modes of thought and that its structure reveal rather than forcibly resolve the contradictions in our lives. UCLA's Bob Rosen, for example, argues that *Salt of the Earth* offers no "cerebral space" that will allow for speculation; that instead of making people think about the issues it raises, it moves them to laughter and tears.[2]

Even some of those who worked on *Salt of the Earth* now concede some truth to these criticisms. The film is a well made story; it has a tight, carefully organized plot that leads to too tidy a dénouement. Evolutions of consciousness are never so ordered in life as the film suggests, nor are resolutions so unambiguously satisfactory. The film's use of the various resources of the medium—camera and editing room, sound track and visual images—underlines its themes instead of complicating them. *Salt of the Earth* knows where its convictions lie, and it openly attempts to engage its audiences' sympathies for them. Consequently, it is at times melodramatic, particularly in the neatness of its happy ending and in its polarization of good and evil along class lines. The bosses and the deputies never transcend cardboard figures, racist capitalist pigs and their agents. That their counterparts were equally nasty in real life is no vindication of aesthetic merit, though it does answer the charge of anti-Communist critics that these figures were exaggerated for propagandistic purposes.

The limitations of *Salt of the Earth* as film art are precisely those one might expect of the product of a group of filmmakers who learned their craft in Hollywood and whose critical theory evolved when radicals were stressing social realism as a mode and workers' lives and struggles as content. The filmmakers' aesthetic was a deliberately affective one; they wanted the film to involve and move its audiences. They would never have shared the concern of some radical critics today—legitimately worried about an excess of sentimentality in our culture—that appeals to the heart might preclude appeals to the mind.

Herbert Biberman's and Paul Jarrico's essay "Breaking Ground" succinctly describes the aesthetic convictions that informed the making of

147

Salt of the Earth.[3] Above all, the filmmakers wanted to make an authentic film about the lives of those whom Hollywood systematically ignored, one that would "by-pass the pitfall of naturalism—a mere surface record of actual events—and emerge with an imaginative work of art that was still true in detail."

On those terms, the film succeeds admirably. It may lack irony and ambiguity, but it has another kind of richness: a density of historical allusion. It recreates the spirit of the strike and many of its events with fidelity; more important, it gives life to the larger patterns of history. Image after image, phrase after phrase (Esperanza's voice-over, for example), condenses whole episodes in the experience of the Mexican-American people in that part of the Southwest: their early presence as tillers of the land and the loss of that land to Anglos and corrupt *ricos*; longstanding patterns of discrimination and resistance to it; the century-long history of labor struggle; even the patterns of cultural and linguistic colonialism.

Though it lacks the tough dialectic of recent Third World films, in which the heritage of the past is at once a source of strength and a road-block to progress, *Salt of the Earth* respects Mexican-American culture without patronizing it. The Spanish language is woven into the texture of the film. References to the *floricanto*—flower and song—add a poetry to the screenplay while evoking the Latino background of the people. Similarly, Sol Kaplan's musical score conveys the Mexican heritage by using variations on "La Adelita," a song of women in the Mexican Revolution. The film suggests, too, the incursions of Anglo culture on the older heritage, especially in the cowboy music played over the radio bought on the draining installment plan. When the deputies take away the radio, they force people to draw on their own capacity to create culture rather than to depend as consumers on prepackaged goods. "Here," says Ramón, thrusting a guitar at one of his friends, "Let's hear some *real* music for a change."

If not venturesome, the film's unobtrusive style seems appropriate to its subject. The filmgoer is aware, not of the camera work and the editing, but of the land and the people. In the mind's eye, images linger: the apprehensive women running toward the mine while the siren warns of an *accidente*; the families gathered by moonlight to serenade Esperanza with "Las Mañanitas" on her saint's day; a sleepy child's face pressed against the bars of the jail; the women dancing on the picket line. Some of this imagery is accessible in the screenplay; that is one of the reasons it is such good reading.

Another reason is the depth and complexity of the central characterizations—Ramón with his bitterness and his love, Esperanza and her slow, hard-won growth. Their estrangements and reconciliations, all too familiar even today, are at the center of Salt of the Earth's dramatic tensions. Yet their relationship, unlike the claustrophobic marital conflicts in recent films like Ingmar Bergman's Scenes from a Marriage, is also part of a larger community. The film shows other couples in that community dealing with problems similar to Esperanza's and Ramón's. It depicts the children as integral to the community's life. And it suggests a broader range of human relationships than the familial alone. Both male and female friendships are important: Ramón takes refuge in the men's culture of the bar; Esperanza's growth arises from and contributes to her growing sense of identity with the other women, her growing sense of responsibility toward them.

Some of the film's best moments suggest in small ways this growth, these changes. One is the moment when Esperanza removes the chair from under Ramón's feet and brings it into the circle for the meeting of the auxiliary. Another is the scene when, in jail, she passes the children quietly to Ramón, then slowly lifts her head, opens her mouth, and for the first time shouts with the other women; perhaps one has to be a woman to know what an important moment that is. In addition to an evolving marriage, the film presents the transition of a women's culture from unity in commiseration to unity in strength and the impact of that transition on the community as a whole.[4]

In doing so, Salt explores the complicated relationship between class struggle and the struggles of women and an ethnic minority. Sometimes the different struggles—against sexism, racism, the unchecked power of the ruling class—conflict with one another, bump contradictorily against one another; sometimes they converge. Where they conflict, the mining community is divided against itself. Where they converge, there is unity. The film moves toward that moment when Ramón says, "Now we can all fight together." Its power as a narrative structure comes largely from its acknowledgment and use of that pattern of conflict and convergence, of division and unity. Fundamentally, the film is about the struggle of the working-class community to unify itself.[5]

The opening scenes establish almost immediately the conflict between the women and the men, between the problems of the women and the problems of the men. The camera shows both Esperanza and Ramón at work—Esperanza chopping wood, carrying it to the fire, scrubbing the clothes, hanging the wash, tending the children; Ramón lighting fuses of dynamite in the darkness of the mine shaft. It suggests the difficulty and significance of both kinds of work. Yet initially the conflict between Ramón and Esperanza centers on their mutual failure to understand the extent and source of each other's feelings of oppression:

> **Esperanza** (timidly): What's more important than sanitation?
> **Ramón** (flaring): The safety of the men—that's more important!

"Have your strike," she concludes in desperation. "I'll have my baby."

Her prediction is fulfilled in the sequence juxtaposing the beating of Ramón with Esperanza's childbirth, unattended by a doctor because none will come to the picket line or treat a striker's wife. Again, the nature of their specific oppression differs, but in calling out for each other they express their bond with each other—a bond of love as well as pain. The cross-cutting underlines, perhaps a little heavy-handedly, the commonality of their struggles.[6] Both learn during the course of the film that, though their needs may differ, they can best demand redress only by joining forces. The difficulty—and a major source of the film's dramatic interest—is that they learn this lesson in different ways and at different rates.

At the point of their greatest estrangement, Esperanza insists on the "indivisibility of equality." She compares her oppression as a woman and the oppression of Mexican-Americans as a racial minority. Her words are at the heart of the film:

> Why are you afraid to have me at your side? Do you still think you can have dignity only if I have none?... The Anglo bosses look down on you, and you hate them for it. "Stay in your place, you dirty Mexican"—that's what they tell you. But why must you say to me, "Stay in *your* place." Do you feel better having someone lower than you.... Whose neck shall I stand on to make me feel superior? And what will I get out of it? I don't want anything lower than I am. I'm low enough already. I want to rise. And push everything up with me as I go.... And if you can't understand this you're a fool—because you can't win this strike without me! You can't win anything without me!

150

Ramón raises his hand to strike her—an exericse of male power obviously familiar if not habitual. She stiffens in defiance, ordering him never to threaten her physically again. "That would be the old way." And she retires to sleep alone. The gulf between the two of them as individuals seems unbridgeable; so, for a moment, does the gulf between the rising of the women and the struggles of the workers in their exclusively male occupation.

Like the divisiveness of sexism, the divisiveness of racial antagonism also figures within the working-class community, though less prominently. Mostly, the film attributes racism to the Anglo power structure, where it emerges, as racism often does, in crude and obvious ways: the designation of Ramón Quintero as "Ray" and "Poncho," his beating in the police car, the statements about the childlike mentality of Mexican-Americans. More subtle is the suggestion of how these antagonisms divide and embitter the workers. Ramón harbors a deep hostility to Anglos, regarding both Frank Barnes and Jenkins with a suspicious eye, blaming "those Anglo dames" for Esperanza's growing involvement in the strike. The film downplays racism among the Anglo workers; Frank Barnes's friendly, educable ignorance is the closest to it. But Jenkins's tale of the bosses' attempted seduction reminds the Mexican-Americans that their white co-workers have one thing in common with the bosses that they will never have—their color.

These tensions in the narrative structure are reinforced by certain key images, though *Salt of the Earth* is not a highly symbolic film. Guns, for example, in addition to serving their literal function, become icons for both a crude machismo and the power of the ruling class. At times this imagery seems almost too obvious, as in the frame filled by the holster and gun on the hips of the deputy Vance, who later taunts the female picketers in an obvious (though entirely believable) *double entendre:* "Hey girls!... Don't you wanta see my pistol?" At times it is more subtle. In the barroom scene when the men are feeling most pessimistic, they find a news photo of the owner of the company, expensively clothed for a safari with his gun across his lap. The men, with the false consciousness that apes the activities of the ruling class as a substitute for genuine power, decide that they too will go hunting, a decision arising directly from their sense of helplessness. During most of the climatic confrontation scene between Esperanza and Ramón, when Esperanza is at her strongest and Ramón at his weakest, most defensive, and potentially most brutal, Ramón clings to his rifle, cleaning, oiling, and loading it for the hunt.

During the hunt, though, a gunshot marks the point of his decisive turn-about. And in the final sequence he half raises his rifle, then thrusts it aside. Literally the action represents his rejection of an individualistic, suicidal attack against the bosses, of the explosive but finally ineffectual anger of some of his earlier confrontations. Through the gradual accretions of meaning, it suggests a rejection of the masculine mystique and of ruling-class methods for maintaining power.

The final sequence of *Salt of the Earth* emphasizes the coalescence of the different struggles. That sequence is literally one of convergence, the physical reflecting the political, as streams of people—men and women, young and old, Anglo and Chicano—pour toward the scene of the eviction. Initially we see only a few people at *la casa de Quintero*, the members of the community of women with whom we are most familiar—Esperanza, Luz, Mrs. Salazar—and the children. Gradually others join them, the women flagging down cars, the men arriving in Jenkins's car and the union truck, the crowd swelled increasingly with still other women walking down from the surrounding hills, with the "guys from the open pit," with "the guys from the mill." The children throw dirt clods at the deputies, an effective diversionary tactic in a general and organic movement of resistance.

In the final frames the camera creates visually the image of unity summarized by Ramón's "Now we can all act together." It lingers on the faces of the crowd gathered to watch and finally halt the eviction. Then it draws back to show the crowd as a solid, dense mass. For a time it focuses on Ramón and Esperanza on the steps of their house—the baby, for the first time by his own choice, in Ramón's arms. The final film image is the people, as they leave the area. The hard-won unity is not permanent, nor is the victory, as Hartwell's "Maybe we better settle this thing—for the present" makes clear. But something significant has been won, an inheritance for the future, a sense of hope and confidence and power to pass on to the children: "And they," Esperanza's final voice-over predicts, "the salt of the earth, shall inherit it." "Esperanza," of course, means "hope."

The power of the conclusion lies not only in the relief of narrative suspense—of knowing that the strike has been won and that the personal relation between Esperanza and Ramón has, at least, "for the present," rejected the old way and advanced to a higher plane of consciousness. It is also powerful as the last tonic chord of a music composition is powerful: relieving a *structural tension*. At last the entire working-class community can all come together in a shared political action, as before it could not; the conflicting claims of feminist, ethnic, and class consciousness are dramatically resolved.

Salt of the Earth's form—a love story moving inevitably toward a happy ending—is traditional. Its characters and concerns are not. Its vision, though, is progressive rather than revolutionary. It does not explicitly urge workers to take control of the means of production, since to do so would have been politically impossible and historically inaccurate; more seriously, it forces a resolution on essentially unresolvable contradictions. It does argue for a strong and democratic unionism capable of wresting better working conditions from those who own the means of production, and it does intimate that winning a single strike is no final victory. *Salt of the Earth*'s feminism also falls short of what feminists today consider radical. Ramón comes to understand how important and demanding household tasks are when he is forced to assume them during Esperanza's three days in jail, but certainly the film offers no criticism of the nuclear family itself and of the basic division of labor along the line of traditional sex roles. Its feminism stops where feminism stopped in the lives of those who worked on the film and lived the history on which it is based. Even so, *Salt of the Earth* is virtually the only film of its era constructed on the premise that women are not the subordinates of men, but their equals.

Twenty years after *Salt*'s completion, a group of French workers and filmmakers set out to tell the story of a strike by women workers in a mill and garment factory. *Salt of the Earth* was one of their models. In their film, *Coup pour Coup (Blow for Blow),* directed by Marin Karmitz, the workers played themselves and engaged in a constant process of criticism and revision of the script. Some of the scenes were shot with videotape and replayed so that the women could assess their authenticity. *Blow for Blow* carries its radical vision beyond the militant trade unionism of its predecessor to argue a vision of spontaneous revolution. The trade union, controlled by the Communist Party, appears as reformist. It has made no demands for child care, has never fought to secure equal wages for women, and offers no possibility for feminist leadership. The protest against the fragmentation of working mothers' lives and the implicit insistence that child care be treated by society as work make *Blow for Blow* an important contemporary sequel to *Salt of the Earth*.[7]

Whatever its limitations, *Salt of the Earth* helped keep alive a tradition of struggle. The objections of modern critics to its melodramatic appeal have some validity. Yet surely there is a place for two kinds of politically committed film art: one that leaves us troubled, speculative, and critical, and one that, like *Salt of the Earth*, gives us hope for the possibility of social change.

NOTES

PROLOGUE

[1] This essay was originally printed in *California Quarterly*, 2 (Summer 1973), 60-63. It is reprinted in this volume, along with other short pieces from that issue.

[2] His name was Lester Balog. He was a retired educational organizer for the United Auto Workers. In the three years I knew him, he drove the hundred-mile round trip between his home and my university every semester to show his worn sixteen-millimeter print of *Salt of the Earth* to my classes. He died not long ago. The attendance and testimonials at his memorial service showed that I was only one of many—Chicanos, older people, farm workers, auto workers, women, educators—who owed him thanks.

[3] Among those who attacked the film were Roy Brewer, international representative of the powerful International Alliance of Theatrical and Stage Employees; California Congressman Donald Jackson; Screen Actors Guild President Walter Pidgeon; syndicated columnist Victor Riesel; Hollywood gossip columnists Hedda Hopper and Louella Parsons; and industrialist Howard Hughes. Hughes's letter to Jackson advising him about ways to suppress the film is included below (pp. 183-84). So are excerpts from a forty-page chronology prepared in May 1955 by Paul Jarrico, *Salt*'s producer, documenting for the filmmakers' attorneys the conspiracy to block production and distribution of the film (see Chapter IV and pp. 185-87). Independent Productions Corporation, the company that co-produced the film, charged some sixty defendants with conspiracy to restrain trade by violating antitrust laws. In 1964, a jury ruled that there was insufficient evidence to prove a conspiracy, and the filmmakers lost their case.

[4] Her review is reprinted in *I Lost It at the Movies* (New York: Bantam, 1966), pp. 298-311.

HOLLYWOOD

[1] When quoted and paraphrased material appears without a full citation, it comes from interviews conducted during 1975-77.

[2] According to Richard O. Boyer and Herbert M. Morais, *Labor's Untold Story* (New York: United Electrical, Radio, and Machine Workers of America, 1955), wages were frozen at a 15-percent increase over 1941 wages, while prices had soared by 45 percent and profits by as much as 250 percent.

[3] According to Peter Biskind, "The Way They Were," *Jump-Cut* (May-June 1974), p. 24, I. F. Stone was the first to point out the influence of these reports, back in 1952. Boyer and Morais discuss them at length. The first of the series, *Communist Infiltration in the United States*, was aimed at the entertainment industry. The third, *Communists within the Labor Movement: Facts and Countermeasures*, laid the basis for the Taft-Hartley Act.

[4] Dramatizations based on the period include, in addition to *The Front*, Eric Bentley's *Are You Now or Have You Ever Been?* (New York: Harper, 1972), culled from his *Thirty Years of Treason: Excerpts from Hearings before the House Committee on Un-American Activities, 1938-1968* (New York: Viking Press, 1971), an essential resource; and the televised drama, *Fear on Trial*, from John Henry Faulk's book of the same name. These dramas, like most of the memoirs from the period, including Biberman's book, focus almost entirely on the outrageousness of the investigations, the sufferings they inflicted, and the question of civil liberties, rather than exploring ideological issues or talking about what people were doing before the blacklists. The same is true of most of the many panels and seminars on the era held over the past two years in Los Angeles—though I am indebted to these discussions for my sense of the period.

Studies of the period are more searching, though often they treat the left either ironically or apologetically. One of the more thorough and dispassionate studies of the investigations into the entertainment industry came out early: John Cogley, *Report on Blacklisting*, 2 vols. (Fund for the Republic, 1956). Cogley himself was blacklisted for his work, presumably for underestimating the seriousness of the red menace. Of recent books on the blacklist, the most thorough and balanced is Cedric Belfrage, *The American Inquisition, 1945-1960* (Indianapolis: Bobbs-Merrill, 1973). Robert Vaughan, *Only Victims: A Study of Show Business Blacklisting* (New York: Putnam's, 1972), has some insights to offer, though his title suggests the book's primary orientation. Stefan Kanfer's *A Journal of the Plague Years* (New York: Atheneum, 1973) is a glib and cruel, though occasionally informative, work. The shorter commentaries I found most helpful were Biskind's article, cited above, and Gary Wills's introduction to Lillian Hellman's memoir *Scoundrel Time* (Boston: Little, Brown, 1976).

[5] Four of my acquaintances are now working on books that will examine more fully the experience and ideas of the Hollywood left than I can do here. One of them will be published by Doubleday around the same time as this volume:

Larry Ceplair and Steve Englund, *Hollywood Screenwriters and Politics, 1933-1955* (tentative title).

⁶ Al Richmond, *A Long View from the Left: Memoirs of an American Revolutionary* (New York: Delta, 1972); Peggy Dennis, *The Autobiography of an American Communist: A Personal View of a Political Life, 1925-1975* (Westport: Lawrence Hill, 1977); Jessica Mitford, *A Fine Old Conflict* (New York: Knopf, 1977). These books make fascinating reading; taken together, they recreate a whole social and political world.

⁷ In writing about this aspect of *Salt of the Earth*'s background, I worried about violating the implicit assumptions, if not the trust, of some of those I interviewed. The decision to do so was in many ways a painful one. But I came to believe that any other approach would be dishonest. As it turns out, my worries were unfounded. I sent drafts of this manuscript to all whom I had interviewed, and no one objected to the openness, though some felt that the emphasis on a left tradition and the Party in particular imposed too systematic an interpretation on the messiness of history.

⁸ Among left critics of the Party are Stanley Aronowitz in *False Promises: The Shaping of American Working Class Consciousness* (New York: McGraw-Hill, 1973) and James Weinstein in *Ambiguous Legacy* (New York: Franklin Watts, 1975). Left historians are waging a vigorous debate about the effectiveness of the CPUSA in the thirties and forties. The main positions in the debate are outlined in articles by James Weinstein and Max Gordon in *Socialist Revolution*, No. 27 (Jan.-Mar. 1976).

⁹ According to Max Gordon, "The Communist Party of the Nineteen-Thirties and the New Left," in the issue of *Socialist Revolution* cited above, 100,000 had joined the Party by the end of the 1930s, with "a network of supporting organizations of at least half a million" (p. 22).

¹⁰ Paul Jarrico speaks of this consistency with a candor facilitated by his long residence in France, where "If someone says, 'Are you a Communist?' it is not a sensitive question. You don't think, 'Oh, my God, why is he asking me that question?' It's just normal." The film, he says, was conceived "by left-wing people who were left-wing before they made it and left-wing while they made it and most of whom remained left-wing after they made it."

¹¹ Peggy Dennis's autobiography, cited above, provides a particularly informative account of the problems of women in the Communist left. It took the women's movement and three different drafts of her manuscript before she was able to confront this issue openly and to her own satisfaction.

¹² For a detailed discussion of Biberman's aesthetics, see George Lipsitz, "Herbert Biberman and the Art of Subjectivity," *Telos*, No. 32 (Summer 1977), pp. 164-82.

[13] Asked about the influences and ties that informed his own politically committed work in film from the forties on, Wexler laughed and said briefly, "We're all old Commies." It was a deliberate oversimplification, but there is an element of truth in it.

[14] *Additional Dialogue: Letters of Dalton Trumbo, 1942-62*, ed. Helen Manful (New York: M. Evans, 1970), pp. 40-44.

[15] The Hollywood left is full of self-deprecating anecdotes about its often ineffective gestures toward "influencing" film content. In one of Paul Jarrico's films, for example, Lionel Stander managed to sing a few bars of the *Internationale* in an elevator on the way to a Christmas party. John Bright, one of the four founders of the Hollywood Studio Section of the Communist party, remarked bitterly to interviewers David Talbot and Barbara Zheutlin, "Non-Communist writers were the ones who got stuff over the screen, social content. The credits of the Hollywood Ten are shameful . . . the purpose of their attorneys [in wanting to introduce their scripts as evidence in the hearings] was to prove there was no social content in anything they did." The study cited in the next note provides a more generous assessment.

[16] Dorothy Jones, "Communism and the Movies: A Study of Film Content," in Cogley, *Report on Blacklisting*, 1:196-304. As Peter Biskind points out in the *Jump-Cut* article cited above, this was the real significance of her study, not her predictable failure to find evidence of "Communist propaganda" in their films.

[17] One of the best analyses of the First Amendment issue was written by Dalton Trumbo while he awaited the outcome of his appeal. It was reprinted with two related essays in *The Time of the Toad: A Study of Inquisition in America* (New York: Harper & Row, 1972).

[18] In 1946, movie audiences had averaged a weekly attendance of between eighty and ninety million. By 1953, they had subsided to forty-six million. By 1948, the employment of actors and writers was at its lowest since the predepression slump. Fewer than one million TV sets had been sold in 1945; by 1950, that figure reached seven and a half million. One survey of four hundred TV families found a decline in monthly moviegoing of 72 percent for adults and 46 percent for children (Kanfer, pp. 75, 81; Andrew Dowdy, *The Films of the Fifties* [New York: Morrow, 1973], pp. 1, 5-6). In addition, the Department of Justice in the late forties abolished price-fixing, blockbookings, pooling agreements, and other forms of industry control over exhibiting theaters, weakening the monopolistic control the major studios had exercised over virtually every aspect of production and distribution. Charles Higham gives a full account of the twenty years of hearings leading to this decision in *Hollywood at Sunset* (New York: Saturday Review Press, 1972), pp. 18-32.

[19] Columnist Ed Sullivan succinctly explained the industry's capitulation: "Wall Street jiggled the strings; thas all" (Kanfer, p. 77). Actually, as Kanfer points

out, the financial interests of Wall Street and those of the major studios are essentially the same. He lists the ties of RKO, headed by Howard Hughes, with the United Fruit Company; of Atlas Corporation with the National Can Company; of Twentieth-Century Fox with General Foods, Pan American Airways, New York Trust, and National Distillers; of Warner Brothers with J. P. Morgan and American Power and Light. In *The Time of the Toad* Trumbo traces Johnston's contradictory public statements from an assertion that he will "never be a party to anything as un-American as a blacklist" to the "Waldorf Statement" (pp. 19-22).

[20] Jarrico verifies this account in John Cogley, *Report on Blacklisting*, pp. 107-108.

[21] Quoted in Herbert Biberman, *Salt of the Earth: The Story of a Film* (Boston: Beacon, 1965), pp. 299-300. His book contains long excerpts from the trial transcript.

[22] Hollywood has never exactly welcomed controversy in film content. The Production Code Administration, created by the Motion Picture Association of America in 1934, allowed the industry to police itself by reviewing and approving films meeting its standards. As film historians point out, the P.C.A. ensured that most commercial features would be declarations of faith in our particular social system. (See, for example, Leif Furhammer and Folke Isaksson, *Politics and Film*, trans. Kersti French [London: Studio Vista, 1971].) Still, films had been far more adventuresome in other eras.

[23] The study is Jones's "Communism and the Movies," cited above. Jones points out that the hunger for light entertainment is reflected in the choices of the Academy of Motion Picture Arts and Sciences for best film of the year: *All about Eve* in 1950; the musical *An American in Paris* in 1951; *The Greatest Show on Earth* in 1952. In 1954, a fine and powerful film, *On the Waterfront*, made a clean sweep of industry honors—but its message is essentially antiunion and an informer is its hero. Its director, Elia Kazan, had testifed as a friendly witness before HUAC.

[24] For example, Congressman Richard M. Nixon's query of Jack Warner, "I would like to know whether or not Warner Brothers has made, or is making at the present time, any pictures pointing out the evils of totalitarian communism..." (Quoted in Trumbo, *Time of the Toad*, p. 49).

[25] *Popcorn Venus* (New York: Avon, 1973), pp. 259, 264-65. Rosen is one of many cultural critics to point out that the feminine mystique of the fifties replaced a far more generous conception of women's roles and personalities. In the forties, with the country at war, the men away, and women in the millions working as crane operators, truck drivers, factory hands, and miners, women had appeared in films, advertising, and popular fiction in a variety of roles with a variety of strengths. But Johnny came marching home in 1945, and by 1947, more than three million women had been laid off. The fifties had no room for Rosie the Riveter.

158

[26] *Hollywood Review*, 1 (June–July 1953), pp. 1, 3–4. The continuity of belief underlying such an analysis emerges perhaps most fully in a work of film criticism also published in 1953, *Film in the Battle of Ideas* (New York: Masses & Mainstream) by playwright, screenwriter, critic, and scholar John Howard Lawson, another of the Hollywood Ten. Lawson, first president of the Screen Writers Guild and former head of the Hollywood Studio Section of the Communist Party, includes a section called "The Degradation of Women." His analysis attributes the negative images of women in films entirely to the economic interests of industry under capitalism. Today his analysis seems simplistic and even sexist; yet at least he was asking people to look at the ideological assumptions reflected in women's roles.

[27] For a fuller description and interview, see Victoria Hodgetts, "The Odyssey and Comeback of Gale Sondergaard," *The Village Voice* (August 2, 1976), pp. 93, 100–101.

[28] *Official Proceedings of the Forty-Ninth Convention of the International Union of Mine, Mill, and Smelter Workers*. St. Louis, Mo., 1953, pp. 84-85.

NEW MEXICO: THE BACKGROUND

[1] Much of the descriptive and factual material in this section has been synthesized from the following sources: Carey McWilliams, *North from Mexico: The Spanish-Speaking People of the United States* (New York: Greenwood Press, 1968; reprinted from the 1948 edition); Matt S. Meier and Feliciano Rivera, *The Chicanos: A History of Mexican Americans* (New York: Hill and Wang, 1972); Vernon H. Jensen, *Heritage of Conflict: Labor Relations in the Nonferrous Metals Industry up to 1930* (Ithaca: Cornell University Press, 1950); and various publications of the Silver City–Grant County Chamber of Commerce and of the Kennecott Copper Corporation, Chino Mines Division, particularly the pamphlet "This Is Chino." Other sources consulted include Warren A. Beck, *New Mexico: A History of Four Centuries* (Norman: University of Oklahoma Press, 1962); Art Preis, *Labor's Giant Step: Twenty Years of the CIO* (New York: Pioneer, 1964); Julian Samora, ed., *La Raza: Forgotten Americans* (Notre Dame: University of Notre Dame Press, 1966); George I. Sánchez, *Forgotten People: A Study of New Mexicans* (Albuquerque: Calvin Horn, 1967); and Stan Steiner, *La Raza: The Mexican Americans* (New York: Harper & Row, 1969).

[2] Elguea's heirs, for example, continued to control Santa Rita through their manager Don Juan Ortiz.

[3] Jensen, *Heritage of Conflict*, p. 9.

[4] It was reopened by one Martin B. Hayes, who had obtained a shaky title to the claim now known as the "Chino" (Chinaman) claim. But Indian attacks continued, shipping costs were high, and the smelting furnace he had built was in-

adequate. Hayes sold the mine to J. Parker Whitney. At the turn of the century some men from New York took over operations. The Chino Copper Company was formed in 1909, the mill at Hurley erected in 1911.

⁵ In all the tensions between rich and poor, Anglo and *mestizo*, a source of particular bitterness was land ownership. The Treaty of Guadelupe Hidalgo in 1848 had guaranteed the property rights of Mexican-Americans, but the tangle of Anglo-Saxon laws, based on a system of ownership totally different from the Hispanic, made Mexican-Americans frequently the prey of Anglos who often occupied the best agricultural lands. In the 1870s and '80s, an alliance of Anglo politicians and some wealthy Hispanic families known as the Santa Fe ring took over millions of acres, depriving many Mexican-American small farmers of land their families had owned for generations. The process continued into the nineties, with the creation of the Court of Private Land Claims, most of whose judges, of course, were white. The history of early land grants made proving title extremely difficult, and often the original grantees lost their holdings under the letter of the law. Eventually Anglos came to hold four-fifths of the grants. Mexican-American residents of New Mexico today still recall the loss of those lands with anger. That loss is an important subtheme of *Salt of the Earth*.

⁶ Some vivid descriptions of life in the mining towns of the Southwest are in Agnes Smedley's autobiographical novel, *Daughter of Earth* (Old Westbury, N.Y.: The Feminist Press; reprinted from 1929 edition). Of Tercio, in New Mexico's Sangre de Christo range, Smedley writes:

> Over Tercio brooded the same atmosphere as in Delagua, smoldering discontent and hatred. Here were the same complaints about the weigh boss, the hours, wages, insufficient props and other precautions against falls, the high prices and dishonesty of the Company store, the payment of scrip instead of American money. The miners dragged themselves to the holes in the mountainside each morning, and . . . dragged themselves home at night. . . . To these miners . . . existence meant only working, sleeping, eating what or when you could, and breeding. For amusement there was the saloon for the men; for the women, nothing. (pp. 117-18)

⁷ The living condition of peons in Mexico just before the 1910 revolution was desperate. Working for less than twenty cents a day, deprived of land increasingly concentrated in the hands of a few rich hacienda owners, many sought work for American companies both south and north of the border.

⁸ Even in the 1880s, some unionizing among Mexican-American workers took place—for example, the organization of the Caballeros de Labor, patterned on the Knights of Labor; this group concentrated, unsuccessfully, on combatting the land-grabbing schemes of Anglo capitalists.

The development of trade unionism in the hard-rock mines paralleled the increasing industrialization of the mines, requiring ever larger capital outlays and ever larger work forces of semiskilled and unskilled workers, and the increasing formation of trusts and consolidations among the mining companies. The publicity from Kennecott's copper-mining division proudly records its own process of consolidation. Formed in 1909, the Chino Copper Company merged with Ray Consolidated Copper Company in Arizona in 1924, then with Nevada Consolidated Copper in 1926. In 1933, Chino, Ray, Nevada, and Utah Copper—all initially established by Daniel C. Jackling of Utah—became part of Kennecott, which had been incorporated in 1915 to mine copper in Alaska. The Braden Copper Company in Chile also became part of the conglomerate. The publicity does not mention the growing class antagonism between workers and owners.

[9] They also mirror contemporary labor history in general: the great movements for the eight-hour day; the development of an industrial unionism to oppose the craft unionism of the American Federation of Labor; the formation of the Western Federation of Miners; and the massive resistance of employers to workers' organizations through vigilante action, deportations, the employment of unscrupulous Pinkertons, the mobilizations of National Guards.

[10] Meier and Rivera attribute to the WFM an "ability to develop union leadership among the Mexicans..." (p. 170). Historian Miguel Casillas, in "Agitation or Discrimination: A Reappraisal of the Clifton-Morenci Strike of 1916-1917," an unpublished paper delivered at the Second Annual Southwest Labor Studies Conference in Spring 1976, argued, on the other hand, that the WFM frequently ignored and often exploited Mexican-American workers.

[11] General information about Mine-Mill locals in New Mexico's central mining district comes from Lucien A. File, "Labor Unions in New Mexico's Nonferrous-Metals Mining Industry," reprinted by the New Mexico Bureau of Business Research (October 1964), and from interviews with Clint Jencks.

[12] Another important figure in the events leading to the strike was Robert Hollowa, once a cellmate of Tom Mooney's, then a regional organizer for Mine-Mill and a tough and fiery radical.

[13] Even moderates like New Mexico Governor Edwin Mechem cautioned workers not to assist "the spreading doctrine of a slave state." In a radio address over Silver City station KSIL in July 1951, Mechem argued for a speedy settlement of the strike, based on an understanding between "the two necessary groups comprising our capitalist system—labor and management... in order that we may support our defenders in uniform with the bullets they need to do the job" (as quoted in the Silver City *Daily Press*, July 28, 1951, pp. 1-2).

NEW MEXICO: THE STRIKE

[1] Material about the strike comes from two main sources in addition to interviews: the Silver City *Daily Press* and the *Union*, official organ of the International Union of Mine, Mill, and Smelter Workers. It was an interesting exercise to compare the coverage of the two; the *Daily Press* became increasingly hostile to

the strikers as the strike wore on and as its editorial policy moved increasingly into the pro-McCarthy camp.

[2] EZ's management took the position that because zinc-mining was smaller-scale and less profitable than copper-mining, EZ could not afford to be as generous as the copper companies. The premise of that proposition is true; the conclusion, debatable. The price of zinc rose from $13.88 per hundred in 1950 to $17.50 in 1951. New Jersey Zinc paid stockholders $4.96 a share in 1950, $6.00 in 1951. The Silver City *Daily Press* of January 4, 1951, carried the headline "New Record for Zinc Use Set; Production Highest Since 1943." The year the strike ended, 1952, was again a peak year for lead and zinc in the state, production totalling $19,185,000. Empire Zinc paid its stockholders some of the best dividends in the industry. (The statistics are from the speech by Governor Mechem cited above and from Beck, p. 249. The figures in the New Mexico Mining Association, Bureau of Mines and Mineral Resources pamphlet, "Your Underground Resources," differ slightly.)

[3] The *Daily Press* of August 17, 1951, carried the report verbatim.

[4] The movie, of course, could not include every event of the strike. One which must have been as lively as the day in jail occurred just over a month later. Several hundred men and women sympathetic to the union accompanied its leaders to court in Silver City. There they descended en masse on Sheriff Goforth, occupying his office and demanding that he fire the two deputies responsible for some of the more reprehensible instances of violence. They also staged a mass rally on the lawn of the Grant County Courthouse, chanting "No Marshall Law" and "Fooey on Foy." A Silver City doctor complained that two of his patients, who must have been very sick indeed, were thrown into convulsions by the noise.

[5] Both the Silver City *Daily Press* and the *Union* carry extensive accounts of the entire episode. Even the *Daily Press* is implicitly critical of the strikebreakers' violence.

[6] The Bayard-Silver City community seems to have been divided about the strike. Some Bayard businessmen and town board members, including the mayor, signed petitions sympathetic to the strikers. Opponents countered with a petition of their own, accusing the strikers of having pressured the sympathizers into signing. Most threatening, vigilante groups began meeting at the Grant County recreation center, muttering about taking the law into their own hands.

[7] Evictions play a large part in the mining community's consciousness, particularly a mass eviction in the early thirties. According to oral tradition Bayard got its start when miners living close to the open pit mine at Santa Rita on land leased from the company were ordered to leave, ostensibly to make room for expansion. It seems the company's desire to enlarge the pit coincided with its concern over some militant union-organizing by workers in the mine and smelter. The evicted workers moved their houses to the flats between Santa Rita and Hurley,

where Tom Foy, a wealthy Anglo rancher, was rapidly selling small plots at large profits.

⁸ Particularly heinous levies were the "peace bonds" the courts began to require of arrested picketers and leaders. The union decided to test their constitutionality, and Vicente Becerra, on the negotiating committee, remained in jail for twenty days when he refused to post a five-hundred-dollar bond. When attorney David Serna filed a motion to appeal, Justice Haugland reduced the bond to two hundred and fifty dollars and released Becerra.

Even the Grant County Bar Association got in on the anti-union litigation. When International officer Maurice Travis accused EZ during a radio broadcast of having "bought" an injunction, saying that the law enforcement machinery of the county was owned lock, stock, and barrel by the companies, Bar Association president C. C. Royall vowed to punish the union for casting such aspersions on the legal system and filed charges of criminal contempt against Local president Cipriano Montoya, Clint Jencks, and Travis.

⁹ As cited in the Mine-Mill *Union*, October 12, 1953.

¹⁰ The government prosecuted Matusow for "perjury" after his recantation, and he served five years in federal prison. His book *False Witness* (New York: Cameron and Kahn, 1955) makes interesting reading.

¹¹ *The Mine-Mill Conspiracy Case* (Denver: Mine-Mill Defense Committee, 1957), p. 16.

¹² It was not until the Taft-Hartley indictments that the membership of some of Mine-Mill's officers and organizers in the Communist Party became generally known. It was in such instances that the secrecy of membership was especially damaging. "Exposures" of key figures as Communists guaranteed dissension among the members of progressive unions and left many of them with the feeling that they had been manipulated.

¹³ Maurice Travis, then secretary-treasurer of the International, insisted in a 1977 interview that the leadership of Mine-Mill had reservations about the strike and the making of the film at the time. "We had enough trouble already," he said. He himself supported the project in spite of his reservations. My sense is that this is one instance in which the Communist Party did play an important role, instructing its members in Mine-Mill's leadership to support the making of the film.

THE MAKING OF *SALT OF THE EARTH*

¹ (Boston: Beacon, 1965), p. 27.

² Interviewed at her home in Cuernavaca, Revueltas recalls, "When I read the script I said, 'Well, I'll do this picture if this is the last thing I'll ever do.' It was. Since then I haven't been able to work again in Mexico." Revueltas worked

for three years in the late fifties with Bertolt Brecht's theater company in East Germany. She returned to find herself still *persona non grata* in the Mexican film industry. Originally a dancer, she teaches ballet today at a studio on her grounds. She has no regrets about having done the film.

[3] *Official Proceedings*, p. 86.

[4] In his book, Biberman says that when insufficient personnel and equipment mandated the use of a stationary camera, he decided to shoot scenes from the same angle but at a number of distances. This way the pace of the film, with its unprofessional cast and their slow, halting English, could be speeded up by rapid cutting; and "because there were no changed angles, the audience would not have a sensation of abruptness and being yanked about" (*Salt of the Earth, The Story of a Film,* p. 80). Hurwitz and his assistant Joan Laird say that this was an after-the-fact rationalization for static camera work.

[5] Later Hurwitz worked on the editing of the film at a cutting room built secretly in Topanga Canyon, until further differences again led to his departure. Ed Spiegel and Joan Laird did most of the editing.

WE, THE WOMEN

[1] *Official Proceedings*, p. 64. Braulia Velásquez and Virginia Chacón both addressed this convention to tell the story of the women's picket line.

[2] Probably too much of the experience of the women of New Mexico, as I tell it in this chapter, comes filtered through the perceptions of Anglo men and women. Some of the women from the New Mexican community had left the area and were impossible to track down; some were clearly reluctant to talk to me—an Anglo woman asking questions about events still controversial. I believe the account here is factually accurate, but nuances in interpretation and emphasis might have been different had I been able to speak with more of the Mexican-American women from the central mining district of New Mexico. I did speak at length with five of them—Virginia Chacón, Fina Marrufo, Mariana Ramírez, Anita Torres, and Esperanza Chacón Villagrán; my debt to them will be clear.

[3] Of the five women from New Mexico interviewed for this study, four assented in various ways to this summary. The fifth, Virginia Chacón, is more angry, less optimistic in her assessment of change.

[4] An Anglo woman's view of the status of women in small New Mexican mining towns around the turn of the century is suggested in the following passage from Smedley's *Daughter of Earth,* mingling compassion and some racial bias of its own:

> The man of the house was a Mexican on the school board...and he felt it his right, as a man and as an official, to talk at length with the most intellectual woman in the countryside. And that woman was I! His wife was a

broad, good-natured Mexican with no ambitions and no ideas. He always ate his supper with me and she waited table, moving back and forth from the kitchen to the room which was the dining-room, the living-room, and my bedroom, all in one. Later, she and her child ate their supper in the kitchen.... I dared show no sympathy with the woman... such would have been a deadly insult to the man.... (pp. 129-30)

[5] Mariana Ramírez thinks that the company persuaded the priest to include this warning in his sermons. Picking up her husband at 11:30 one night after the late shift in the Hurley mill, she saw ahead of her the manager of Empire Zinc. She followed him to the priest's house, where he went inside. That Sunday the priest threatened to excommunicate any woman who went to the picket line.

[6] Some of the women were involved in support for the strikes and organizing drives of the middle and late forties; Virginia Chacón, for example, remembers soliciting food and donations house to house during a 1946 strike at Phelps Dodge in Tyrone. But such involvements were sporadic until the "Salt" strike.

[7] Clint Jencks speaks of a "common consciousness of common problems" as having grown out of the organizing efforts of those years, and no doubt he is right. Yet the consciousness seems to have extended more in one direction than the other: toward acquainting the women with the men's problems in the mines and smelters and enlisting their help, rather than toward acquainting the men with the problems of the women in the home.

[8] Lest anyone conclude that sexism was limited to New Mexico, listen to Stanley Babcock, delegate to Mine-Mill's 49th Convention in 1953, representing a local in Butte, Montana, long a center of progressive working-class militancy. When he spoke before the auxiliary there, says Babcock: "Some of my good friends... afterwards cussed me and told me to keep my nose out of it, that they didn't want their women in an auxiliary" (*Official Proceedings*, pp. 28-29).

[9] "Mine-Mill Women Organize Backing for Union's Struggles," *World Trade Union Movement Fortnightly Review*, 10 (May 1952), p. 18. The "opposition" included women from the other union. The women of Bayard, too, seem to have been particularly angry at the women who opposed them, the wives of scabs.

[10] Progressive Miners of America was a left-wing union engaged in bitter rivalry with John L. Lewis's United Mine Workers of America.

[11] "First Annual Report" of the Illinois Women's Auxiliary, Progressive Miners of America, 1933, pp. 8-12.

[12] *Official Proceedings*, p. 26.

[13] Ironically, Montoya shot and killed his wife several years later when she became involved with another man.

[14] The resolutions were as follows:

Therefore, be it resolved:

(1) That the union locals make some tangible expression of appreciation to the wives of active union members whose everyday lives are affected greatly by their husbands' participation in union activity;

(2) That when issues arise in the community or the nation on which the union takes a position and decides on a course of action, that the union locals consider how women can be involved in such a campaign and utilize this vast source of potential energy.

(3) That a section of the *Union* and the local union papers be directed toward women and written for them, explaining to them the current issues of especial interest to women and informing them of the activities of women in support of the union.

(4) That union locals encourage and organize activities for the whole family.

(5) That a campaign be undertaken to popularize *Salt of the Earth* in written form preparatory to the showing of the film, that every effort be made to ensure that as many men and women as possible see the film, and that we call on our women to assist us in doing a job on this in the various communities.

(6) Since the need for a tremendous amount of work amongst women is evident, and since there already exists, in the Ladies' Auxiliaries of the International Union of Mine, Mill, and Smelter Workers a corps of women whose understanding of and loyalty to the union has been amply demonstrated;

Therefore, be it resolved; further:

(a) That we call on the Ladies' Auxiliaries to assist us in carrying out the tasks outlined.

(b) That at the same time union locals give every assistance and cooperation in building and strengthening organizationally the Ladies' Auxiliaries where there are such, and where none exist that immediate steps be taken to organize a local auxiliary.

(c) That the International Union and the union locals concerned take special steps to bring into union activity the women of the two large minority groups within our union, the Negro and Mexican-American women who have already shown that they have a tremendous contribution to make.

(d) That the International Union continue to give cooperation and financial assistance to the Ladies' Auxiliaries and try to give more attention to the problems of leading and organizing this body of union women.

(e) That the Executive Board of the International Union be requested to give serious consideration to the appointment of an organizer or organizers for the Ladies' Auxiliaries and thus ensure that adequate attention will be given to the problem of strengthening the support amongst women for the International Union of Mine, Mill, and Smelter workers. (*Official Proceedings*, pp. 27-28)

[15] The part-time, temporary appointment of an organizer for one local in British Columbia at the munificent sum of fifteen dollars a month was considered significant enough to merit a story in the *Union*; but the International never did appoint a permanent organizer for the auxiliaries. The *Union* contained responsible enough reportage on the activities of the auxiliaries in the next couple of years; but then, it had always aired an article or two on the subject and I saw no evidence of a sustained increase in consciousness about a women's audience or "women's" issues.

[16] The woman question did enter by the side door in Clint Jencks's trial. Defense attorney John McTernan asked unsuccessfully for a change of venue from El Paso on the ground that the composition of the jury panel was unconstitutional "by reason of systematic exclusion of half the citizens of the country—women." When asked on the stand if names of women were put into the box from which the jury panel was drawn, Jury Commissioner Stevens replied, "Never knowingly."

SALT OF THE EARTH: A CRITIQUE

[1] "A Response to Kate Ellis's 'Women, Culture, and Revolution,'" *The Radical Teacher*, 1 (June 1976), p. 9.

[2] Rosen ventured this opinion at a discussion session on Ideology and the Media featuring Stanley Aronowitz. Both concurred in their criticisms of the film, though finding it "engaging." I disagree with their assessment of the film's merit but I am indebted especially to Rosen and to students in one of his classes at UCLA for many of the ideas in this chapter, particularly the brief discussion of the film's iconography and the concept of a pattern of conflict and convergence, though they never applied that pattern specifically to *Salt of the Earth*.

[3] For a fuller discussion see the *Telos* article by George Lipsitz, cited above (chapter I, note 12).

[4] Ellen Cantarow gives a lucid account of that transition in the essay quoted at the beginning of this chapter. Cantarow applies Sheila Rowbotham's description of "a protective, defensive women's lore" to the women's culture before the strike—"sharing the bitterness of raising children while material and emotional resources are scarce." "The strike," she says, "changes this: the ruts of earlier habit become the paths toward class and feminist consciousness, and revolt."

5. In *False Promises* Stanley Aronowitz writes that the "contradiction of working-class struggle today is that it must recognize the demands of different oppressed groups...and simultaneously strive for a unified class identity that transcends the prevailing system" (pp. 333-34). Though Aronowitz faults *Salt of the Earth* as art, the statement could have been written to summarize its politics.

6. Some of the women in the New Mexico community, comments Virginia Derr Chambers, objected to this sequence, because it equates the natural pain of childbirth with the unnatural torture of Ramón. The important point is that Esperanza had no medical assistance; not that she experienced the pain of childbirth.

7. This assessment owes much to Julia Lesage's discussion of *Coup pour Coup* in "*Tout Va Bien* and *Coup pour Coup*: Radical French Cinema in Context," *Cineaste,* (Summer 1972), pp. 42-48.

Barbara Kopple's *Harlan County, U.S.A.,* winner of a 1976 Academy Award for the best documentary of the year, deals superbly with material similar to *Salt of the Earth*'s.

MAKING THE FILM

Contemporary Accounts

BREAKING GROUND

by Paul Jarrico and Herbert J. Biberman

I.   When our company was formed two years ago, we were agreed that our films must be based in actuality. Therefore, we were entering an arena of art to which we as craftsmen brought little experience and in which we found little precedent to guide us. It was clear that the best guarantee of artful realism lay not in fictions invented by us but in stories drawn from the living experience of people long ignored by Hollywood—the working men and women of America.

And so we searched for stories that would reflect the true stature of union men and women. We dug into material dealing with minority peoples, because we believed that where greater struggle is necessary, greater genius is developed. We looked for material that might record something of the dynamic quality women are bringing to our social scene.

Salt of the Earth, originally the third project on our schedule, seemed the best embodiment of the elements for which we had been striving. A true account of the miners of the Southwest and their families, predominantly Mexican-Americans, begged to be told without the hackneyed melodramatics which so often destroy honesty in the name of excitement. It was not the many abuses and hardships suffered by these

The four short articles reprinted here were originally published in *The California Quarterly*, volume II, number 4, Summer 1953. That same issue of the journal also included the screenplay of *Salt of the Earth*.

169

people that loomed so significantly out of the material—it was their humanity, their courage and accomplishment. We decided that these Americans, at once typical and exceptional, could best be realized on the screen by the simplest story form of motion picture: a love story of two mature and decent people.

Michael Wilson, author of the story, had come to know these New Mexico miners during a long and bitter strike they waged against a powerful zinc company in 1951 and 1952. The story idea was born out of his first visit there, and he then wrote an extended outline, or, in movie parlance, a treatment of the story. Mr. Wilson returned to the mining community with this treatment, where it was read, discussed and criticized by a score of miners and their wives. With this guidance in authenticity he proceeded to write the first draft screenplay. When it was completed, again we followed the procedure of group discussion and collective, constructive criticism. By rough estimate, no less than four hundred people had read, or heard a reading of, the screenplay by the time we commenced production.

Perhaps it was our determination that the people in this film be life-size that led to our second decision. We asked the miners and their families to play themselves rather than be enacted by others.

These decisions brought the writer, director, crew and cast face to face with intricate problems of realistic form and content. How could we by-pass the pitfall of naturalism—a mere surface record of actual events—and emerge with an imaginative work of art that was still true in detail? How could we best blend the social authenticity of documentary form with the personal authenticity of dramatic form? What range of characterization should be given individual roles whose enactment would be undertaken by non-professionals? How could we capture the quality of speech of these bilingual people and yet make the picture completely intelligible to an average English-speaking audience? How could we make the amazing heroism of these people not only stirring, but *believable* and *inevitable?*

This last problem was particularly important to us, because only if we solved it could our picture help engender in an audience a belief in its own capacities, a confidence that what these people had done could be done again. We hoped that our film might become a cultural stimulus to other trade unions and minority groups, and convince them that they could tell their own stories through the medium of film.

170

High hopes! And vast problems. Certainly we cannot boast of having solved all these aesthetic questions. But we do think we have broken new ground. If our film can illuminate the truth that the lives and struggles of ordinary people are the richest untapped source of contemporary American art, and if it can demonstrate that such films can be made by these people themselves, then it will have achieved a basic purpose.

II. It is against this background of intention and dedication that the attacks upon this picture during the course of production must be seen. We had been shooting *Salt of the Earth* since January 20th, Inauguration Day. The production was sponsored by the International Union of Mine, Mill and Smelter Workers, and our cast included hundreds of its members and their families. Even after a storm of hysterical publicity burst over us, thousands of our neighbors and associates in the Silver City area assumed we had a right to be there.

A false assumption, said Congressman Donald Jackson. On February 24th, this California Representative delivered a speech in the halls of Congress, in which he said:

> ...Mr. Speaker, I have received reports of the sequences filmed to date...This picture is deliberately designed to inflame racial hatreds...[It] is a new weapon for Russia. For instance, in one sequence, two deputy sheriffs arrest a meek American miner of Mexican descent and proceed to pistol whip the miner's very young son. [They] also imported two auto carloads of colored people for the purpose of shooting a scene depicting mob violence.

As a direct result of Congressman Jackson's speech, our leading lady was arrested, members of our cast and crew were physically assaulted, and a vigilante committee warned us to leave "within twelve hours or be carried out in black boxes." We defied the deadline, demanding and receiving the protection of the New Mexico State police, and finished our work on March 6th. After we did depart, however, and the protective police as well, the attacks on our Mine-Mill brothers and sisters continued. Two union halls were set afire, one of them burning to the ground. Also razed by arson was the home of a union leader, Floyd Bostick, who had played a role in the film. His three young children narrowly escaped the flames.

Without reading the script, or asking to, without seeing the film, or waiting to, an incendiary Congressman had spoken.

His fury can be understood only if one recognizes how unprecedented it was for manual workers and cultural workers of our country to collaborate, and what promise for a more truly democratic future such a collaboration holds. In organizing for independent production, we had one basic aim: to place the talents of the blacklisted (both those who had worked in films and those who had never been given the opportunity) at the service of ordinary people. There were indeed Negroes in this production: an assistant to the director, an assistant cameraman and two technicians—all in categories of work never available to Negroes in Hollywood.

Simon Lazarus, a respected motion picture exhibitor, had formed Independent Productions Corporation to back us. Money was borrowed from liberal Americans, it being understood that none of us who wrote, directed or produced the film would receive any remuneration until the loans were repaid.

In the wake of the Silver City storm, Mr. Lazarus was himself hailed before the Un-American Activities Committee and asked to divulge who the backers were. He refused to answer personal questions and thus could not be forced to inform on others. He did, however, volunteer to tell the Committee what our film was about. But the investigators were not interested. They did not want to investigate, but to prejudge and censor.

The efforts to prevent *Salt of the Earth* from being made began long before the spectacular assaults in Silver City, and continued long after our location shooting was completed.

Consider, as a pre-production problem, a crew. In Hollywood, most motion picture technicians belong to the International Alliance of Theatrical and Stage Employees (AFL). West coast head of the IATSE is Roy M. Brewer, who inherited his protectorate over Hollywood labor from two gangsters, William Bioff and George E. Browne. A zealous adherent of Congressional witch-hunters, Brewer has understood that his civic responsibility to enforce the blacklist goes far beyond his trade union responsibility to see that his men get jobs. That, no doubt, is why he refused to let us hire an IATSE crew. As a trade paper reported it later:

Simon Lazarus, named as prexy of the company, approached Roy M. Brewer, the chairman of the AFL Film Council, about nine months ago, seeking assurance from him that he could make a motion picture using the "Unfriendly Ten." Brewer yesterday recalled he flatly told Lazarus he would prevent such a project in every legal way possible. — *Daily Variety, February 25, 1953*

"Legal" was an afterthought. What Brewer said was that he would see us in hell first.

We gathered a union crew despite Roy Brewer. Some were members of his own IATSE. Some had been expelled from the IATSE for opposing Brewer's rule. There were Negroes, denied membership in the IATSE because of its Jim Crow policies. Every member of our crew carried a union card.

As for post-production problems, the would-be censors of the picture have tried to sabotage it in every way. They have demanded that all laboratories close their doors to us, warned technicians not to help us— lest they find themselves blacklisted. Failing here, we expect they will extend their intimidation to film exhibitors when the picture is ready for release. Meanwhile, Congressman Jackson has been needling the Departments of State and Commerce to find some obscure statute which might forbid the export of this picture. No such statute exists, but we would be naive to think that the legality of our endeavor will give the bigots pause.

III. Will the film be shown? We have no illusions about the fight that lies ahead. Of this we are certain—the harrassment will continue, and we will need many allies to defeat the censors and saboteurs. Naturally, the degree of support we eventually get will depend on the end product—the finished film. If trade unionists someday discover that this picture is the first feature film ever made in this country which is of labor, by labor and for labor; if minority peoples come to see in it a film that does not tolerate minorities but celebrates their greatness; if men and women together find in it some new recognition of the worth and dignity of a working class woman—then this audience, these judges, will find ways of overcoming the harrassment.

But to reach these judges, we must first get past the *pre-judgers*.

To reach these eventual allies, we need immediate allies—for whether the people are to praise this film or damn it, they must first have the right to see it. That is why we appeal to everyone who is morally concerned with free communication to help provide the atmosphere and the place in which *Salt of the Earth* can be shown and judged on its own merits.

REFLECTIONS ON A JOURNEY

by Rosaura Revueltas

I don't remember much of that flight from Mexico City to Ciudad Juárez. As the plane droned north toward the border, I was oblivious of the passengers around me, completely absorbed in my thoughts of the experience that lay ahead—the making of *Salt of the Earth*. I had waited so long to do this picture; production had been postponed several times because of various difficulties—but now at last I was on my way to Silver City.

In a way it seemed I had waited all my life to do this picture. My own mother was a miner's daughter. As a child I learned of the miners' hardships, their joys and sorrows; and I grew up wondering why these people on whom the wealth of nations depended were among the worst paid workers in the world. From the day I became an actress I longed to play a role that would honor my people. And now such a role had been offered to me—for these miners of New Mexico were *my people*, even though they lived across the border.

The plane droned on. I closed my eyes and thought of Esperanza, the miner's wife I was to portray in the picture. I was still thinking of her when we landed, and took the airport limousine to El Paso.

There were several Mexican students with me in the limousine. At the border we handed over our documents to the U.S. inspector. He glanced at our vaccination certificates, seemingly the only thing that interested him, returned our documents and waved to the driver to proceed. That was all.

I spent the night in an El Paso hotel, and the next morning, when checking on my plane reservation to Silver City, showed my papers to the airport clerk to make certain that they were perfectly in order. It seemed a little strange to me that my passport had not been stamped at the time of entry. I was assured that this technicality was of no importance; I could always prove my date of entry with my validated airplane ticket, as well as the fact that I had crossed the border in an airport limousine with other passengers (whose passports also had not been stamped).

So I gave the matter no further thought. From the moment I stepped off the plane at Silver City, to be met by a delegation of miners' wives, I was engrossed in the creative work before us. Even when the first attacks against our picture appeared in the press I felt no danger to my own status. We were within a week of our goal when two agents of the Immigration Department visited the lodge in Silver City where the cast and crew were staying. They wanted to see my passport. I showed it to them. In their cold, polite manner they told me they needed to inspect it and would return it to me in a few days.

Work on the picture went forward as usual for the next three days. On the fourth day, returning to the lodge from our location set, I found the same two agents waiting for me. This time they had a woman with them—a matron. They had come to arrest me on the grounds that my passport lacked an admission seal. They told me it was nothing serious, that I could return to work the next day if a $500 bond were posted in El Paso. Nevertheless, they forced me to leave immediately in their car, without dinner, and all the way to El Paso they kept interrogating me. Was I a Communist? Weren't the people I was working with Communists? Wasn't this a Communist picture? For the first time I began to feel frightened. Not for myself, but for the picture. Some powerful man or men were out to kill our picture.

Paul Jarrico, our producer, had followed us to El Paso in his car in order to post my bond. But no sooner did the authorities see that I was about to go free again than they revoked the original warrant of arrest, issuing a new one that stated I was to be held without bail.

That first night I was installed in a hotel room, and two guards set their chairs right outside my door. For the next ten days and nights these two "shadows" or their replacements never left me. I drew small comfort from the thought that this arrangement was preferable to jail. In a way, these shadows made the situation more ominous; I had committed no crime, yet I was their prisoner nonetheless.

But by the time of the first hearing I had regained my hope of an early release. I had great confidence in my attorney, Mr. Ben Margolis, and felt that as long as I had him at my side nothing could go wrong. But the first bad sign was the exclusion of my friends from the hearing. Many of them had come from Silver City and other towns, and although the hearing was supposed to be public, they were not admitted. Then, in the hearing itself, I saw my attorney win argument after argument and yet lose on the basic plea—that I be released on bond pending a formal judgment on my status. And I began to realize that the forces trying to stop the completion of our picture were more powerful than I had imagined.

Those last days in El Paso I recall only as a confused and evil dream. There were other hearings, protests, appeals—much of them in a legal jargon I didn't understand. But this much I did understand, and remember:

I heard a government attorney describe me as a "dangerous woman" who ought to be expelled from the country. At other times he referred to me as "that girl." Since he had no evidence to present of my "subversive" character, I can only conclude that I was "dangerous" because I had been playing a role that gave stature and dignity to the character of a Mexican-American woman. . . .

I remember the face of the government attorney, or "prosecutor" I guess you would call him, and the nervous smile that contorted his lips, and the way his hands trembled. And I thought it strange that he, who represented Law and Authority, should be so frightened—while my friends in Silver City, who were undergoing intimidation and violence, were not nearly so scared as he. . . .

Perhaps that is why I did not feel a sense of defeat when the decision was made that I return voluntarily to Mexico. My attorney and friends still believed that I would be vindicated in the higher courts—but a further appeal would take time. Meanwhile, production in Silver City had been completed except for a very few scenes involving me, and the company could not afford to keep the crew waiting indefinitely for my release. And so I agreed to re-cross the border.

It wasn't a happy leave-taking. There were bitter memories I could not leave behind. But I also carried home with me the spirit that had made this picture possible, the determination that would see it completed, and the inner assurance that a handful of ignorant and frightened men could never prevent its being shown to the peoples of the world.

ON LOCATION

from a Crew Member's Diary, by Jules Schwerin

Silver City, Jan. 13, 1953. Flew in from El Paso Sunday...this is a beautiful country of rugged mountains, semi-arid tableland and the bluest sky I've ever seen...weather is ideal for shooting now but old timers here say it's capricious and we may have snow or wind-storms without warning....

Jan. 16th. The miners and their families have given us a warm welcome...for them it has been a difficult year, waiting for this picture to get under way...some of them doubted that they would ever get to tell their story, but now it can be told, by *them*, playing themselves....

Jan. 20th. Most of the crew has arrived...I am struck by the remarkably high level of capacity of these men, many of them distinguished technicians with long records of outstanding achievement...the relationship developing between the crew and the miners is a wonderful thing to watch...a real spirit of brotherhood, each group learning from the other...every day more miners pitch in to help the crew, some of them after a grueling eight-hour day in the mines. Our construction team can take pride in the fact that the miners find our mine-head set authentic. They are amused by the film technique of building "wild" walls and partially constructed rooms, but they are quick to catch on to all the technical phases of movie-making....

Jan. 21st. The first scene with dialogue was shot today, the scene of the beef between the mine foreman and the men. Everyone was tense. One miner kept muffing his lines. He apologized, explaining that the actor-foreman reminded him of a real foreman he had known, and added: "He gets me so damn mad I forget my lines." If we can sustain this kind of reality, a few muffed lines won't matter....

Jan. 30th. The local theatre was filled yesterday with union people, coming to see the first "rushes" of the picture. When the mining families saw themselves on the screen, they howled and cheered and laughed ...it was a catharsis...many of them tell us now, "we're not going to be alone anymore." And we of the crew know how deeply they feel this and are glad we are with them....

Feb. 4th. We're having real difficulty in casting "Anglo" roles. Two remarkable men have been cast as the principal deputy sheriffs in the picture. They are friends of the union, and hate to play these parts, although recognizing the necessity of someone being a heavy. They resent wearing the garb of the typical deputy, lest some union man mistake them for the real McCoy. Casting strikebreakers is even more difficult. "Anglos" sympathetic to the miners simply don't want to play these roles, while those who are "neutral" are afraid to sign up for work as extras lest local employers accuse them of being sympathetic to the union.

Feb. 10th. Our schedules must undergo daily changes to accommodate for the mobilization of actors, particularly in mass scenes. Most of the families have no telephone service...distances are fantastic...they live in various mining communities, ten, fifteen, twenty miles apart...organizing a baby-sitting-and-jitney-service for a hundred people is really something...and it would be impossible without the Ladies' Auxiliary of the union...we are all impressed by the stamina and courage of the women and the relaxed nature of their children...as a result of the strike, the women have moved closer to equality in the home and a fuller participation in union affairs. The results of that victory are seen now in the way women assume responsibility for matters formerly reserved to men....

Feb. 16th. Despite the provocations and slanders of Congressman Jackson and the local vigilantes the community is surprisingly calm ...many people in Silver City in no way connected with the union continue to offer us gratuitous services...the Catholic priests have been friendly and helpful...the union men say they expected these attacks would come...what a marvelous experience to work with such confident, courageous people!

Feb. 20th. Attacks on the picture are becoming more vicious... the local union-haters are beginning to mutter about mob action...tradespeople in Silver City who have been friendly to us are starting to retreat a little...some of those who have extended service to us are receiving anonymous threats by telephone....

Feb. 24th. It isn't enough that we're in the vortex of a political storm whipped up by creatures who don't know what the picture is about —even the weather's against us. A snow blizzard swoops in on us, and trying to be flexible, we adapt the scene to shoot it with snow. Suddenly the sun comes out and the snow melts before we can even get a master scene. So we return to the original plan. Suddenly a wind storm comes up that makes the set look like the Gobi Desert. And so it goes....

Feb. 27th. Immigration agents arrested Rosaura last night. As they led her off, we all stood around feeling angry and helpless, and tried to act brave and unconcerned, assuring one another that she would be back tomorrow...but today we all worked harder than ever, with a new zest and a new grimness...the bond between the crew members and the union cast is stronger than ever...nothing can stop us now from finishing this film...our responsibility is great....

March 1st. The union has decided to send Joe Morales to Washington to state the union's case, to see what can be done to stem the hysterical flood of lies, free Rosaura, and restore law and order...Joe, a charter member of the local, was chosen unanimously in a most unusual meeting, which was held on location, while shooting of the film continued in a nearby ravine...the meeting lasted all afternoon, with men slipping away from the deliberations to take their places before the camera ...and because a few important voices were missing, the plan was submitted to one of the brothers who was sick at home, and another at work in one of the mines...conducted in the most parliamentary manner, this meeting was a demonstration of direct democracy...militant miners acting with calm and assurance, aware of the historic importance of what they had undertaken....

March 4th. Today is "super-patriot's" day in Silver City. The vigilantes' campaign of intimidation is at last having its effect on the business community. All morning the loud-speaker in front of the leading theatre blared martial music, and toward noon the doors were opened for the showing of an anti-communist movie. All commercial establishments in town were "advised" to close shop and attend the movie—or *else*. All the same, stores kept their side doors open—to us....The flag-waving hoodlums are threatening to lynch us, our star is still under arrest, and the weather stinks. So what do we do? We keep right on shooting the picture.

March 6th. The production is finished. We have a complete picture, except for a few shots of Rosaura...maybe when the picture is cut the editor can find a way of getting by without those shots of her...It was difficult to say goodbye. The usual guitar, the usual song, the usual laughter were absent. There was almost a fear of looking at one another —a look might have to start a farewell...the last scene was completed and our crew turned to face the miners and their families, our brothers and sisters, and all our affection, all of our admiration and respect for each other was shown in our embraces and unashamed tears...we had shared so much together, learned so much together...I hope that when the film is seen it will bring something of this closeness and understanding to other people....

UNION MADE

by Juan Chacón

When our Union set out to make a movie about the lives of our people, most of us had an idea it might be attacked. My father has a little farm in this County, and I was born there. A lot of our great-grandfathers worked the mines here in the Southwest and had little farms of their own. My people, the Mexican-Americans, have tended the big crops, built the railroads and dug the ore that makes all this big, bare looking country so rich today.

In our Union here, Local 890 of the Mine, Mill and Smelter Workers, a lot of old timers remember the twelve hour day in the dusty wind of the open copper pit, or the heat of the underground zinc mine—twelve hours for two or three dollars a day. They remember the way the companies built houses for the Anglos while we were given shacks with water outside and no comforts inside except what we made with our own hands. They remember the way the miners who spoke Spanish would be put to work as "helpers" to the "skilled" Anglos—doing the same work for which the Anglo was paid twice as much. They remember the separate pay windows, separate washrooms, the separation even in the movies.

My own company, Kennecott, now admits this was the way things were, but they say, "Our policy has changed. Now it's separate, but equal." But don't ever believe it. There's no such thing as "separate but equal."

I never dreamed of being before a movie camera, much less of being a leading actor. But I was willing to play the role of Ramón in *Salt of the Earth* because this picture would give the world at least a little of the background of our past conditions. But this picture isn't *against*—it's *for!* It shows what we can do when we organize and we and Anglo workers organize together. The companies around here have always been afraid of Anglo-Mexican unity. For a hundred years our employers have played up the big lie that we Mexicans are "naturally inferior" and "different," in order to justify paying us less and separating us from our brothers.

Salt of the Earth helps to expose that lie. It shows that workers can get along regardless of religion, color or politics. It shows the gains we have made through the work of our Union. We don't have separate pay-rates anymore, and now we can move up to skilled jobs except where the craft unions keep us out. A lot of segregation still exists, because here in Arizona Kennecott keeps our housing apart from the English speaking miners—and that keeps a wall between us. They even have our kids go to different grammar schools.

But thank God for our Union and for the men who organized it. Back in the thirties, they were blacklisted, thrown off company property, and told to take their houses with them in thirty days or else. The funny thing is that's how the town of Bayard was born. Bayard was a junction in the highway and the jobless Spanish speaking miners dragged their wrecks here and started all over again. Later our Mine Mill Union won recognition and reinstatement for these workers. But what I meant was funny is that today Bayard is the center of the attack against our Union— and it all comes from some Anglo-American business men who settled here to "service" the town we built.

Since those early organizing days we have had many struggles for equality, the longest and bitterest of which was a recent strike against a zinc mining company that lasted fifteen months. The company seemed determined to make this strike a test, a show-down, an attempt to drive us "back into our places." When the company saw it couldn't starve us out, after eight months on the picket line, it got its anti-picketing injunction from a judge here. That's when our wives took over—and it was their idea. We finally won that strike, thanks to the courage and devotion of our women folks.

No movie in the world could tell the full story of those terrible months—and *Salt of the Earth* was not intended to be a documentary record of that particular strike. But I will say this—it is a true account of our people's lives and struggles.

One thing our picture won't show is the fun we had making it. And the headaches. After all, none of us here knew beans about movie making. But we did manage to lick most of our problems. Here's how we did it:

We organized a Production Committee composed both of people from the local union, the Ladies' Auxiliary and the motion picture company. This committee took up everything: the feeding of hundreds of people on the set, publicity, transportation, baby-sitting, equipment. But that was not all. This committee was a policy-making body, with the responsibility of seeing that our picture ran true to life from start to finish. Occasionally there were meetings in which the union people pointed out to our Hollywood friends that a scene we had just shot was not true in certain details. When that happened we all pitched in to correct the mistake. Most of these mistakes were made because the movie craftsmen had not lived through all our struggles; but they had all the heart and the good will in the world and that is how we managed to stand together and overcome the difficulties of making a movie with little money and many amateurs.

One of the most surprising things to us was that we found we didn't have to "act." El Biberman, as we came to call him, was happiest when we were just ourselves. So after a while, we stopped pretending and then, from the "rushes" we saw, the movie began to look better. We even picked up some Hollywood slang and got so we weren't surprised at all when El Biberman said, "Magnificent! Do it again!"

In making this picture we've shown again that no attacks or falsehoods can break our Union spirit, our willingness to work for what's right. We hope our picture will lead the way for other unions to do the same thing. Movies are the main form of entertainment for most people. That's why we figured the big-shots in the movie industry and the mining industry must have something in common—the need to keep alive the big lie about people. If ordinary people told their stories on the screen, think how the walls between us would be broken down! *Salt of the Earth* is our attempt to break through. We hope you see it.

MAKING THE FILM

Documenting the Opposition

LETTER FROM HOWARD HUGHES

March 18, 1953

Congressman Donald L. Jackson
House Office Building
Washington, D.C.

Dear Congressman Jackson:

In your telegram you asked the question, "Is there any action that industry and labor in motion picture field can take to stop completion and release of picture and to prevent showing of film here and abroad?"

My answer is "Yes."

. . . Before a motion picture can be completed or shown in theaters, an extensive application of certain technical skills and use of a great deal of specialized equipment is absolutely necessary.

Herbert Biberman, Paul Jarrico, and their associates working on this picture do not possess these skills or the equipment.

If the motion picture industry—not only in Hollywood, but through-out the United States—will refuse to apply these skills, will refuse to furnish this equipment, the picture cannot be completed in this country.

Biberman and Jarrico have already met with refusal where the industry was on its toes. The film processing was being done by the Pathe Laboratories, until the first news broke from Silver City.

But the minute Pathe learned the facts, this alert laboratory immediately refused to do any further work on this picture, even though it meant refunding cash paid in advance.

Investigation fails to disclose where the laboratory work is being done now. But it is being done somewhere, by someone, and a great deal more laboratory work will have to be done by someone, before the motion picture can be completed.

Biberman, Jarrico, and their associates cannot succeed in their scheme alone. Before they can complete the picture, they must have the help of the following:

1. Film laboratories.
2. Suppliers of film.
3. Musicians and recording technicians necessary to record music.
4. Technicians who make dissolves, fades, etc.
5. Owners and operators of sound recording equipment and dubbing rooms.
6. Positive and negative editors and cutters.
7. Laboratories that make release prints.

If the picture industry wants to prevent this motion picture from being completed and spread all over the world as a representative product of the United States, then the industry and particularly that segment of the industry listed above, needs only to do the following:

—Be alert to the situation.
—Investigate thoroughly each applicant for the use of services or equipment.
—Refuse to assist the Bibermans and Jarricos in the making of this picture.
—Be on guard against work submitted by dummy corporations or third parties.
—Appeal to the Congress and the State Department to act immediately to prevent the export of this film to Mexico or anywhere else.

Sincerely,
Howard Hughes

CHRONOLOGY OF EVENTS

The following excerpts are direct quotations from Paul Jarrico's 1955 chronology, except for explanatory comments in brackets.

Mar. 19, 1953—Congressman Jackson has printed in Congressional Record letters he has received from Howard Hughes, Roy Brewer, and officers of the Commerce and State Departments. These letters constitute a public blueprint of the conspiracy to destroy our property.

[Over the next few weeks, seven laboratories either ignored the filmmakers' registered letters requesting their services in processing *Salt* or rejected the requests outright.]

April 1, 1953—Secret cutting room established at secluded house in Topanga Canyon.

June 28, 1953—Move cutting room to a closed theatre in South Pasadena, still trying to maintain secrecy. Work proceeds, primarily in ladies' room of theatre.

July 18, 1953—Move cutting room to a small, vacant studio in Burbank, still trying to maintain secrecy.

July 21, 1953—Barton Hayes quits as chief editor.... We receive confidential information that Hayes has told the executive board of the editors' local of IATSE that he has worked on "Salt" in order to provide information about our product to the FBI.

During Oct., 1953—We continue putting film through various laboratories under various pseudonyms.... General Film Laboratories recognizes the actual identity of some of our film and refuses to continue working on it, ordering us to remove it from their premises.

Nov. 17, 18, and 19, 1953—Full orchestra under direction of Sol Kaplan records music for "Salt" at Reeves. Neither musicians nor Reeves technicians are told the true identity of the film. (The secrecy under which we felt compelled to work prevented our having the advantage of projecting the film while recording the music for it.)

Nov. 29, 1953 thru Dec. 7, 1953—Re-recording done at an inadequate sound studio in Los Angeles with an insufficient number of IATSE sound technicians. So fearful are they of reprisals by the IATSE and the motion picture industry that they will work only in utmost secrecy, primarily in the dead of night.

During Dec. 1953—Since no experienced negative cutter has been found, members of our regular editorial staff proceed with negative cutting. They are not qualified to handle the specialized problems involved and make many errors.

Summary of Post-Production Period

Work that normally would take three or four months has taken more than a year. Approximately $100,000 . . . has been added to budget.

Feb. 13, 1954 (approximate date)—Tentative agreement reached for our rental of the Squire Theatre for world premiere of "Salt."

Feb. 18, 1954 (approximate date)—Just as the contract for the Squire is to be signed, Zipperman and Fingler [the operators] back out of the deal. We are told privately that they have been fightened by the pressure of the major motion picture distributors. [Jarrico lists five other exhibitors in New York who expressed appreciation for *Salt* but refused to book it.]

Mar. 2, 1954—Sign contract with Philip Steinberg to exhibit "Salt" at the 86th Street Grande Theatre starting Mar. 14, and at the New Dyckman Theatre starting Mar. 26. . . . During the following days representatives of the major motion picture distributors with whom he normally deals tell him he may have trouble booking future pictures if he honors his contract with us. Steve d'Inzillo, Business Representative of the Projectionists Union (Local 306, IATSE) tells Steinberg his theatres may be stink-bombed if "Salt" is played, and hints the possibility of physical violence against Steinberg.

Mar. 9, 1954—The first of five press previews scheduled at the Preview Theatre is held at 11:00 A.M. When invited guests arrive for second showing at 3:30 P.M., IATSE projectionists refuse to run film, acting . . . under instructions of their union. . . . We are not only forced to cancel that screening but five other screenings scheduled at the Preview Theatre.

Mar. 15, 1954 thru April 10, 1954—Despite good reviews and excellent business, no other New York exhibitors ask us to book the film, and we can find no distributor willing to handle it nationally.

May 12, 1954 thru Aug. 11, 1954 (approximate dates)—Every metropolitan paper in Los Angeles, with the exception of the *Daily News*, refuses our ads.

May 13, 1954 thru May 25, 1954—Major motion picture distributors refuse to allow us to book their short subjects to play with "Salt." . . . Even the United Nations Film Commission withdrew a short they had promised us.

May 19, 1954—National Americanism Commission of the American Legion is reported to have put out a special edition of its publication, "The Firing Line," declaring "Legionnaires Must be on Guard Against One of the Most Vicious Propaganda Films Ever Distributed in the U.S."

July 3, 1954—"All Out for All-American Day" in Silver City area. Attended by Roy Brewer, Seaborn Collins, Chairman of American Legion's Security Commission, Actors Anne Doran and Pedro Gonzales-Gonzales, as a demonstration of Hollywood's opposition to "Salt."

During Sept., 1954—Film has short run at the Guild Theatre in Menlo Park, California. . . . This was the last theatrical booking the film had in the U.S. to date. . . . Its total theatrical distribution in the U.S. has been limited to two theatres in New York, one in Los Angeles, one in Silver City, one in Arvada, one in La Habra, and seven in Northern California.

ABOUT THE AUTHORS

Michael Wilson

was an Academy Award winning screenwriter. The films he scripted include *Five Fingers, A Place in the Sun, The Bridge on the River Kwai, Lawrence of Arabia, A Friendly Persuasion,* and *Planet of the Apes.*

Deborah Silverton Rosenfelt

is professor of women's studies and director of the women's studies program at San Francisco State University. She is the author and editor of books and articles on women's studies and women writers, and is on the editorial board of *Feminist Studies.*

A NOTE ON THE DESIGN

The photographs used to illustrate the screenplay
are enlargements of frames from the film itself.
Some were supplied by Paul Jarrico. Others were
made with assistance from the audio-visual
department of the State University of New York
at Old Westbury. Mary Mulrooney of
The Feminist Press coordinated the research and
printing of the frames.

The typeface used for the text of this book is
Compugraphic Souvenir, adapted by Ed Benguiat
from the face originally drawn in 1914 by Morris
Fuller Benton. The text was set by Myrna
Zimmerman, New York, New York.

The display face used is Typositor Busorama, from
Set to Fit, Greenwich, Connecticut.

CPSIA information can be obtained at www.ICGtesting.com
Printed in the USA
LVOW10s1047130515

438331LV00002B/9/P